GHOST STATIONS™

5

by

Bruce Barrymore Halpenny

L'AQUILA

GHOST STATIONS™ *by Bruce Barrymore Halpenny* ©

This New Edition - first published December 2008

British Library Cataloguing in Publication Data
Halpenny, Bruce Barrymore
1. Great Britain. Royal Air Force. Aerodromes. Ghosts.
2. Paranormal. Mysteries. Supernatural

ISBN-10: 1-871448-14-X   ISBN-13: 978-1-871448-14-6
L'AQUILA is an imprint of the **ANZIO Group**

Published by: **ANZIO Group**

                   Greetwell Place
                   2 Limekiln Way
                   Greetwell Road
                   LINCOLN
                   Lincolnshire, England
                   LN2 4US   www.anzio.co.uk

NOTICE: ANZIO Group *does not accept unsolicited manuscripts*

CONTENTS

GHOST STATIONS™ Acknowledgements

My very special thanks to all who have helped me with the books in the **Ghost Stations™** Series ... those who have talked freely about their ghostly encounters - some for the first time - others who have enriched and filled out old stories in my files. Many, many thanks to all those who have loaned me material and photographs and those who so kindly gave me **exclusive** material and photographs to use as I wished. A special mention for my loyal friend Lord Ancaster; also Peter Tory of the Daily Express and the Daily Mirror who prompted me to use material collected over the years when researching for my books **Action Stations 2** Military Airfields of Lincolnshire and the East Midlands; **Action Stations 4** Military Airfields of Yorkshire; and, **Action Stations 8** Military Airfields of Greater London**,** and write the ghost/mystery book which, with demand from the public for more, became then eight books in the **Ghost Stations™** Series:

Lord Ancaster, John Ainsworth; Allan Allchurch; Mr F.W.E. 'Rik' Appleyard; Richard Allen; Wing Commander H. R. Allen, DFC; Wing Commander David Annand; Mrs. Armstrong (née Bevan); Mr M.J. Arnold; Flight Lieutenant Thomas J. Attrill; Mr R. Austin; Mr P. Avis;

Lord Balfour of Inchrye, PC, MC; Robert A. Bell; Paul Booth; Air Vice-Marshal H. Bird-Wilson, CBE, DSO, DFC, AFC; Mr Ken Billingham; Mrs Ann Binnie; Bob Blunden; Neville Bowles; Mr. J. Brice; Jack Broadhurst; Robert Anthony Brunsdon; Steve Bond; Mrs Joan Brown; Miss Ruth Baker; Mr P. Bennet; Mrs Bowyer; Louise M. Brazier; Mr B. Brennan; Bob Bryan; Mark Bryan; Mr Bob Ballard; Nicholas Bell; Neville Bower; Flight Lieutenant John Brown; Mr J. R. Bushby; Bundesarchiv, Germany;

Mr D. W. S. Chapman; Mrs June Constable; Mr Bill Corfield; Mr Allan Cram; Peter Crowson; Mr Duncan Currie; Squadron Leader Tony Cunnane; Edward 'Herb' Currotte; Mr John McCaughrean; Courtenay; Mrs Vera Chapple; Norman Carless; Mr A. J. Charlton; Squadron Leader John Cole, MBE,CC; Miss Denise Marie Curran; Mrs Beryl Christiansen, USA; R. Coleman; D. A. Cross; Stuart Chapman; Jim Chatterton;

Mr R. C. Daniels; Mr Dennis Davis; Squadron Leader Len Devonshire; Clifford G. Dray; Mr R. Downs; Mr W. Drummond; Dorothy Darwood; Paul Dixon; Mrs Elma Drewry; Wing Commander John H. Dyer; Harry Douse; Ron Day; J. Diamantakos for the Glenn Miller photographs, which were taken by his brother; Betty Dalmond; Mr R. C. Davies; Dennis Davis; David Drew; Squadron Leader Neville Duke, DSO, OBE, DFC; Douglas Durkin; William Deiches - writer and speaker on before Christ History - for permission to quote from the article 'Of Men and Angels'; J.C.Dening; Herr Helmut Dreher, Germany;

Mr. E. A. Easters; J. V. Evans; Mrs Audrey Elcombe; Charles Ekberg; Mrs G. Ettidge; Mark Elliott; Thomas England;

Mrs Alice Farmer; Mr F. Fawke; Mr Bernard Feasey; Squadron Leader Brian Fern; Mr J. L. Fletcher; Robin Fletcher; Syd Frogley; Terrance O'Flynn; Ted Foster; Rosemary Ford; Debbie Francis; Mick Fisher; Captain Laura J. Feldman, The Military Airlift Command, Scott Air Force Base;

Geoff Gardiner; Miss Renee Glynn; Mrs J. Greaves; Mr C. R. Green; Alex Gibson; Colin and Melita Gibson; Peter Giles; Graeme and Janice Garnham; Ralph Gilbert; Stan Galloway; Dr Alan Gauld, Dept. of Psychology, University of Nottingham; Duncan Gray; Mrs Winifred K. Grant; Robert Gray; Mrs Jill Grayson; Janet Gibson; Mrs Joan Goult;

Gareth Hanson; Alan D. Harridence; Mr Derek A. C. Harrison; Mr R. Hawkins; W. Hayes; Mrs Peggy Hayles; Mrs Sheila Heple; Eric Hilton Hewitt; Mr Ian Hogg; Mrs Molly Una Hollis; Stan Holtham; Ex-RAF Sergeant Bernard D. Hughes; Mr E. J. Humphries; Mr Peter Hyde; Bernard Halford; Andrew Hall; Charles Humphrey; Lee Hatfield; Trooper Darryl Hewitt and Carol Hewitt; Geoffrey Hall; Peter Hindley; Mrs Jean Horrocks; Brian Hunter, Rhodesia; Jefrey S. Halik; Mrs Eileen Hodgkins; Heinz von Hahn, Geneve; Werner Hoffmann, Germany; Peter Giles Hull;

Brenda Jackson; Brenda Jenkinson; Mrs R. Jones; Mr E.W. Joyce; Major Robert Keith Jones; Colonel de Jong, Dutch Ministry of Defence; Mr Jack Jones; Ray Jackson; Harry Jury; Alan Jones; Ken Jones; Taffy Jones; Mr & Mrs Jackson;

Mr D. G. Kilvington; Mr G. Kimber; Ian King; Gordon Kinsey; Mr Michael Kelham, MA, Headmaster St. Hugh's School, Woodhall Spa, Lincolnshire; Squadron Leader Ken Kenton; Desmond Keen; Mr J. Keward; Miss Kerry-Leigh Parish, Yeovil;

Mr B. G. Leigh; Ron Lines; Philip Levick; Stephen Lowdon; Gamekeeper Phil Longden; John Langford; Stephen Lewis; Leicester County Council;

Mr Edward (Ted) Marcham; Mrs L.B. McKelvey; Mrs W. Meeson, Wilfred Mills, Mr R.J. Minett; Mrs O. Morton; Neil Mayne; Ministry of Defence, London; Godfrey Mangion, Malta; Mr E.T. Manby; Mrs Carol Marshall; Martin-Baker Aircraft Co. Ltd; Mrs Moor; Wing Commander Martin; Bob McPhie, Founder The Dodo Bird Club, Canada;

Lorimer Dennis O'Driscoll; Mrs Molly O'Loughlin White; Pete O'Brien;

Mrs Dorothy Pickard; Mr Jock Pepper; Mr Norman Pepper; Miss Prudence Pepper; Mrs C. Petre; Archie R. Pratt; Tom Perrott, Chairman of the Ghost Club, London; Bill Perry; David Peel; Harry Pain; Squadron Leader Colin Pomeroy; Captain R. N. Phillips; David Pearson; Peter Phillips; Charles Plumb;

Captain Barry Radley; Adrian Railton; George Rance; Mr Laurence F. Round; Mrs C.A. Russell; Ernie Reynolds; Squadron Leader Derek Rothery; William Reeves; John (Jack) Riley; Adrian Railton; Mr Raynforth; Mrs Reedman; David Rimmer, Chairman, Clwyd Aviation Group; Mr F.A.C. Roper;

Mrs Joyce Schofield; Mr S. Scott; Mr Chas Selway; Mr V. Simons; Mr W.E. Simpson; Cliff Sims; Norman W.T. Skinner; Mr Gordon Slater; Brian Stafford; Mrs V. Summers; Walt Scott; Carl Schulte, Lausanne; James Silver; Derek Smith; Flying Officer Brian Stephenson VR; Edward Stott; Francis A. Smith; Harry Smith; Miss Margaret Sawyer; Jack Smith; Dave Sutton; Dick Sharphouse; M. Sarson; Werner Schmidt, Germany; Frau Schmidt, Frankfurt-on-Main; Sue Smithson, South Africa; Sheila Staves, Australia;

Mrs Mollie E. Tilley; Mary Tock; Frank Thomas, Western Australia; Jim and Molly Thompson; Les Timms; Mrs Sylvia Tucker; John Turner; Lance Tebbutt; Jan Thorpe; Flying Officer Nicky Tilmouth, WRAF; John W. Tilmouth;

Steven Upton;

Alan Waddington; John Roy Walsh; Mr Paddy Ward; Mr R.F. Warren; Flight Lieutenant John Wears; Mrs Shirley G. Westrup; Harry Willmott; Mike Whalley, Editor, Morecambe Visitor; Mr R. Wilkie; Mr E.W. Winkless; Julia Wolfe-Harlow; Mr Bill Wood; Peter Wright; Keith Wardell; Miss J.A. Wilkinson; Mrs Cella

Winstanley; Geoff Whitworth; Denise Williams; Brandon White; William E. Whitehead; Gordon West; Keith Walker; Wilbur Wright;

Jill Yates; Bill and Barbara Young;

I am indebted to the editors of: Air Cadet Journal; Air Force Magazine; Croydon Advertiser Group of Newspapers (G. G. Collard); Daily Mirror - Peter Tory's Diary; Evening Star, Ipswich; Gravesend & Dartford Reporter; Grimsby Evening Telegraph; Lincolnshire Echo; Lincolnshire Standard; Metal Box News - R & D Division Metal Box plc; News of the World (David Gordois); Nottingham Evening Post (Martin Stevenson); Romford Recorder (R. J. Mills); Scottish Daily Recorder & Sunday Mail; Sunday Express (James Kinlay); Sunday Mercury - Birmingham (Peter Mitchell); The Press, Christchurch, New Zealand; Yorkshire Post; Aeroplane Monthly; Airforce Magazine - Canada; Birmingham Mercury; Dodo Club, Station C, Victoria, Canada; Stadtarchive Heilbronn; Die Spiegel; Haller Tagblatt; Flypast Magazine; South Somerset Advertiser; Western Gazette; Western Mail & Echo, for permission to publish the photograph of the haunted restaurant; for their very generous help with request letters, article and permission to quote from published stories. My sincere apologies if I have somewhere quoted from an article or work without acknowledgement, also for photographs. Please contact if one has slipped through my heavy workload.

My special thanks to: Leon Thompson, USA; Neville Franklin - Control Column; Duncan Blair; Mrs Betty Hockey; Ken Border for his help with some of the research; Robin J. Brooks for West Malling photographs; Denny Densham for the articles and for the ORIGINAL tape recordings of the Bircham Newton aerodrome haunting, the ORIGINAL tape-recordings of the Bircham Newton update and of the nights investigation at North Weald aerodrome, and for the ORIGINAL tape-recordings of the investigation at Borley Church, the most haunted church in the world, and, to use as I wish with all the ORIGINAL recordings; Dottore Mario Mignella, Pescara, Italy;

Charlie Chester, Sunday Soapbox Programme; Alex Dickson, Radio Clyde; Keith Skues - Yorkshire Radio Network, Radios Hallam, Viking and Pennine - and Classic Gold Radio; Dennis McCarthy at BBC Radio Nottingham; Hans Plantz for translations; Dave Benfield who sorted out the Glenn Miller photographs; Ted Evans for his military reminiscences and valued help; Mrs Hannah Hunt for the many poems, including 'Breakfast' and 'The long Farewell' with permission to publish as I wish;

David P. Sandeman, Chairman of The House of Sandeman for permission to reproduce the 'Sandeman Don'; my racing friend Harry Coulby; Walter Laidlaw, Scotland; last but not least, my military friend in Germany, Hermann Laage for great camaraderie. Hermann worked hard on some of the later German stories and some of Hermann's stories have photographic proof, which give you food for thought. Let me close with a section from one of Hermann's reports:
"Appropriately enough I am writing you this report at midnight and the bats are bumping against my window. At nightfall the bats start coming out of crevasses or cracks in the hill opposite my house. They live in a sealed tunnel that harboured an underground arms factory of the former NSU Works - the NSU Kettenkrad etc. Now millions of these little Draculas must live there."

The material for all the books in the **Ghost Stations™** Series came from decades – since 1950 – of researching and writing about military aviation. Over the years literally thousands of people have contacted me and assisted me … and to everyone … Thank you

INTRODUCTION

I start **Ghost Stations™ 5** with a very interesting story – which I have solved after a great deal of research - and I do explain the blood. I trust that you will enjoy the Ghost-Rider of Nuthampstead.

Hi … I'm Sid Twyning … Is another very interesting story; and I have yet to fathom it out. I do know, that once you have read the story, it will be often in your mind, for it is a very fascinating … short and sweet … as they say; but this is bewitching. The man in Sergeant Peter Hindley's dream was not over-confident or arrogant; he just behaved with assurance.

Let me know what you good readers think of it; also, if A Step Back In Time had the same effect on any ladies; like it had on my mine who did the proof reading and typing. They are Italian and very sentimental. Let me know which stories you like best; and the ones that brought a tear or two.

If you have any stories … or poems, for by public demand, there will be **Ghost Stations™** Poems; then please get in touch with me and mark for my attention.

Cheers.

Bruce Barrymore Halpenny
Roma
Italia

FIVE SOULS

Seeing as this is **Ghost Stations™ 5** I felt it only appropriate to have the Five Souls Poem, for it sums up rather well the feelings of many and also goes to show the reason in many cases for the restless spirits; indeed, one might have almost said that the poet had read my Official Mythology, had it not been the case that the poem was written in the First World War. The soldiers as well as the general public are always lied to, and not always for their own good, but to protect the personal interests of those in power.

W. N. Ewer wrote this very clever poem, which looks at five very different souls; and yet, are at the end of the day the same and have died for the same reasons. He cleverly shows you that regardless of which side you are on, you are the same and the real ones to blame are shown in the last line of each soul ...

"For those who bade me fight had told me so."

FIVE SOULS

First Soul
I was a peasant of the Polish plain;
I left my plough because the message ran: -
Russia, in danger, needed every man
To save her from the Teuton; and was slain.
I gave my life for freedom-This I know
For those who bade me fight had told me so.

GHOST STATIONS™ *by Bruce Barrymore Halpenny* ©

Second Soul
I was a Tyrolese, a mountaineer;
I gladly left my mountain home to fight
Against the brutal treacherous Muscovite;
And died in Poland on a Cossack spear.
I gave my life for freedom-This I know
For those who bade me fight had told me so.

Third Soul
I worked in Lyons at my weaver's loom,
When suddenly the Prussian despot hurled
His felon blow at France and at the world;
Then I went forth to Belgium and my doom.
I gave my life for freedom-This I know
For those who bade me fight had told me so.

Fourth Soul
I owned a vineyard by the wooded Main,
Until the Fatherland, begirt by foes
Lusting her downfall, called me, and I rose
Swift to the call-and died in far Lorraine.
I gave my life for freedom-This I know
For those who bade me fight had told me so.

Fifth Soul
I worked in a great shipyard by the Clyde;
There came a sudden word of wars declared,
Of Belgium, peaceful, helpless, unprepared,
Asking our aid: I joined the ranks, and died.
I gave my life for freedom-This I know
For those who bade me fight had told me so.

GHOST-RIDER OF NUTHAMPSTEAD

In 1984 Adam Gurney went to look over the old Nuthampstead airfield with an old school friend. Both were great aviation enthusiasts and spent much time at air shows and visiting the old wartime airfields.

It was just turned dusk when they drove on to the old runway and started to look around. Some twenty minutes later, Adam suddenly felt compelled to look into his rear view mirror ... he was mesmerised at the sight of a ghost-like rider on a horse, some distance behind, racing towards them at full gallop. He nudged his friend who turned and glanced at the approaching ghost-rider, then hurriedly locked all the car doors. Then they drove quickly away from the on coming ghost-rider.

The old airfield was now only a ghost airfield with only a few remaining buildings, perimeter track and section of runway, the latter being split by a small area of trees. The sections of runway were in very poor condition thus greatly hampering the getaway of Adam and his friend. After some minutes at high speed, Adam realized the bad runway surface was not doing his car any good; and at the opportune moment, drove around the clump of trees and turned off the car engine and lights, in an attempt, now that it was dark, to shake off the pursuer. After a few moments, with no sign of the galloping horseman rounding the end of the tree line, Adam started the engine and retraced his route. The car headlights lit-up the whole runway for quite some distance; and there was no sign of the galloping horseman. The Ghost-Rider had vanished. But where to? As the only possible ways that the galloping horseman could have gone … were around the trees from the other end … in which case he would have been head on to the car or, across the open airfield towards the village; once again putting him in plain view of the car occupants as it emerged from near the clump of trees.

The only other route for the galloping horseman was back the way it had come, that being towards the wood at the far end of the airfield … but here again … he would have been spotted by Adam and his friend before he had reached cover; unless … it was a Ghost-Rider.

So what connection does an old wartime airfield have with a Ghost-Rider? To try and find the answer we must go back to the beginning.

Construction of the airfield began in 1942; and it was constructed by the American Army as a standard bomber airfield for the American Eighth Air Force. It was sited near; and named after, the village of Nuthampstead. Most of the airfield was built in Scales Park on land that was owned by Baron Dimsdale; and was an area renowned for horse riding. Was this the connection with the Ghost-Rider? It could well be for it was said at the time, a horse-woman rode out daily to watch the building of the airfield; which she was against. Before the airfield was completed in May 1943 the mystery horse-woman had vanished.

The airfield consumed some 365 acres of land, which, was of natural beauty. The Technical Site was situated just west of the airfield near Nuthampstead village. The bomb dump was on the south side. Two T2 Hangars were erected plus the usual living sites which, consisted of Nissen Huts.

The first Eighth Air Force unit to use the airfield was the 55th Fighter Group, and they remained until April 1944. The 398th Bomb Group replaced them; and they flew 195 missions from Nuthampstead, by then the war was over.

Nuthampstead finally closed in 1959. Much of the runways and perimeter track were broken up and the hard-core used to build the M1 Motorway.

In 1988 Miss Kerry-Leigh Parish, also a great aviation enthusiast and, interested in the histories of the wartime airfields, met Adam Gurney; and during conversation about the old airfields, told her of his encounter with the Ghost-Rider at the old Nuthampstead airfield. When told the story she said:

"Finding it rather hard to believe I asked him to take me to the airfield. He was very apprehensive but I eventually persuaded him and we set out one autumn day in 1989.

"We found the airfield with some difficulty and again it was nearing dusk. We drove onto the runway and stopped the car so that he could point out the places relevant to the story. The first thing I noticed was how quiet it was. There was not a sound anywhere on the airfield; in fact, it was unnaturally quiet. The other thing was that I felt totally uneasy and cold. We locked the car doors and drove slowly around the line of trees. As no horseman appeared we got gradually more adventurous and found an old track running parallel to the runway we had just left. We drove along this finding it just wide enough for the car. About level with the end of the trees the track curved into an area resembling a dispersal and, as we could go on further; we turned around and were just about to drive back when the headlights of the car reflected off what appeared to be a puddle of about four feet in diameter.

We pulled up next to the puddle and on closer examination … from the car window … we discovered that it wasn't water; but blood that we were looking at. My boyfriend suggested that it may have been left by poachers; but the blood was very fresh and still wet, also it was too large to have been caused by a poacher resting his kill. The blood was also completely unblemished by animal remains such as fur or hair. Yet again a hasty retreat was beaten."

So no sign of the Ghost-Rider … only a pool of fresh blood. Was it the blood from the Ghost-Rider? When asked Adam said: "The horse and rider looked totally … solid … and normal in appearance, there was nothing ghostly about them. It was the way it felt.

"In the fading light of dusk, the rider of the horse was basically just a silhouette; and the details of the rider's clothes were indistinguishable. On sighting the horse and rider my over-riding feeling was one of intense fear."

So the Ghost-Rider could have been either a man or a woman. Was it the woman who was seen in the area at the time the airfield was being built?

But what about the pool of blood? How does that fit into the picture of the Ghost-Rider? Had the Ghost-Rider been wounded? When I asked Kerry-Leigh about the blood she said:

"The blood was sighted on the edge of a perimeter track leading to a pan-handle dispersal at the southern side of the airfield. The blood looked real in every respect and was a vivid red." And she added: "Upon recollection, the fact that the blood had not soaked into the grass at the edge of the perimeter track was very unusual."

And when asked how they felt about Nuthampstead airfield, Kerry-Leigh replied:

"On his subsequent return to the airfield with me, Adam was apprehensive and on edge all the time; and when the blood was sighted, all he wanted to do was leave immediately. My own recollection is of an intense feeling of cold fear and I felt extremely uncomfortable and nervous.

"Of many airfields containing control towers, old accommodation and technical buildings, we have had the feeling of not being alone. There is also an overwhelming quietness that shrouds old airfields. However; Nuthampstead is the only airfield which puts us both ill at ease and it gives you an impression of there being something wrong, every time you visit."

Maybe that is the purpose of the Ghost-Rider … to keep people away … and the blood was the second warning from the Ghost-Rider of Nuthampstead, who I name in the next paragraph.

It is interesting to note – and told here by me, Bruce Barrymore Halpenny and published in this book for the first time – that Thomas Dimsdale, a great horseman and horsemanship … better known as Baron Dimsdale; English physician, twice visited Russia to inoculate the Empress Catherine and others; and for this service received a sum of £10,000 and an annuity of £500.

His works included The Present Method of Inoculation for the Smallpox, (1767), a highly infectious and contagious eruptive fever; said to have been the cause during the 18th century of one-tenth of the total mortality. Jenner announced his smallpox vaccination in 1798 … well after Baron Dimsdale; who was first.

The galloping horseman is Baron Dimsdale … he is the Ghost-Rider; and it is easy to understand why.

We needed the likes of Baron Dimsdale to make us great. Today – in 21st century Britain – Smallpox, TB, Measles etcetera are rampant and out of control. No wonder we have so many restless Spirits.

Baron Dimsdale's beautiful land was taken and it was all for nothing. Brigadier Powell always said: "Do a deal with Russia." We should have done so.

The blood? That is no problem for a skilled physician – one skilled in the art of healing – and this once green and pleasant land called England … does need healing.

A STEP BACK IN TIME

The following supernatural incident happened on the Island of Guam, the largest and southern most of the Mariana Islands in the West Pacific Ocean. The native Guamanians, ethnically called Chamorros, are basically of Indonesian stock. In addition to the official vernacular, English, they speak a distinct language called chamorro.

Now you may ask. What has this got to do with Germany? Let me explain. It is a fact that the Germans were the first to start work on the Atom Bomb; and before the outbreak of war the Wehrmacht had started a research programme to develop the Atomic Bomb. However, never mind how, but the British and American scientists produced it first but the war in Europe is over before they can drop it on Berlin … its intended target from day one … and instead, they drop the first one on Hiroshima, Japan on 8 August 1945.

In 1947, Leon Thompson, then an 18 year old medical-surgical technician with the American Air Force had his posting for Germany, to help with the vast number of prisoners and general health of those recovering from many years of war, suddenly his posting was changed to Japan with the Far East American Air Force and, he went via Guam and it was on Guam that he had a supernatural experience and recalls the happening in his own words:

"I had travelled by sea to the Island of Guam and was to be there until they found a place to ship me, as I was a medic-surgical technician and just out of Medical School from Randolph Field in San Antonio, Texas; so I landed on the island of Guam in mid-June 1947 and, since there was no space available for us Medics' they had us sleep or billet in the old PoW camp where the Japanese held American prisoners of war during the Second World War. I found that island life was not for me. It was too hot and I felt as if I was being roasted alive in those hot days; and we had to get out of the PoW compound and walk about a mile to the mess hall to eat our meals.

"One day, I was late and took a short cut through the jungle, which we were forbidden to do because it still had Japanese snipers on the island, but I took the chance, and as I was going through the jungle, I came upon a building that was western style, and I could hear an old victrola playing records, and the one I heard was Shirley Temple singing "On The Good Ship Lolly Pop Is a Sweet Trip ..." so I walked to the door which was open and looked inside. It was a library and had books on shelves and a beautiful Guam Island woman at the counter, but no one else in sight. So I walked in and she had a large container of pineapple juice all iced down and cold, and the best pineapple juice I ever tasted. She had me sign the old visitors log and we began to talk as she played the old hand-wound victrola.

"Time simply stood still, and I asked about whom she was and as I drank my fill of the pineapple juice, she told me about life on Guam during the Japanese occupation. She told me how the Japanese army made all of the educated people line up and go into a cave, where the Japanese simply took them one by one and cut their heads off; however, one of the teachers who had her head sliced, was still alive, and after darkness others helped hide her from the Japanese army.

"She told me about how some American ships were sighted in the area and late evening at twilight, the Japanese shot down six of their own zeros thinking they were Americans attacking the island. As she talked, I took a good look at all the library books, they were all pre-World War Two but still in good condition. She told me how she used to hide from the Japanese and how they brutalised the natives into forced labour and just killed outright a good number of them just for the fun of doing something.

"Suddenly, I realised I had remained too long. I grabbed my mess kit and took off running through the jungle to the mess hall; but by the time I arrived, it was closed and there was no one around ... as it turned out. I must have spent two hours talking with this beautiful young woman, so I returned to the PoW camp by the long way back and found that they were getting search parties ready to search for me just as I arrived back at the PoW compound, and did I ever get chewed out.

"After I explained to the sergeant in charge, he told me there was no such building on the island, and he and four other soldiers went with me to see the library in the jungle that I had spent so much time in. Oddly enough we searched and searched but no one ever found the building, and I was so perplexed that we could not find the building, I simply could not understand it, because I had been in it and it was there in the jungle, but none of the searchers found anything ... not even a foundation for a building.

"A lot of the guys laughed and said I suffered from the heat, but I know I visited that library and I signed the visitors log. I took a lot of ribbing from the others for two weeks and then came orders to ship out to Tokyo, Japan from Guam. I was standing at the airfield getting ready to board the transport aeroplane for Tokyo, when a jeep came driving up with the sergeant and a captain, and they both called me out of line to speak with me. They wanted to know about the library I had visited and I told them everything; then the captain told the sergeant to get two books out of the jeep, and he brought the books over and asked me if I had seen them before. I looked and sure enough there was the ledger for visitors that I had signed, so I showed them the one I recognised and the sergeant said: "You are a damn liar, these books have been under lock and key for several years."

"I looked so stunned that the captain asked me which page I had signed and I told him I thought it was page 32 ... but, not sure. He opened the old ledger and thumbed to page 32. There in clear visible ink, was my very own signature! The sergeant and captain both looked at each other, then they looked at my signature, and even the date was next to my name, but all of the others were names with dates before World War Two or I should say ... "Pearl Harbour."

"At that moment, the pilot of the transport gunned his motors and I was literally pulled into the aeroplane and the door locked and we took off for Tokyo, Japan.

"The pilot came back and asked what all the hold up was. I explained it to him and he looked at me in a stunned expression. He then asked me everything but the time of day and all about the young woman at the library. What she wore and how she looked, what we talked about and then he pulled out his wallet and took a small photo from it. There was the woman at the library and I smiled and knew I had seen her; then, he looked at me as if he did not know what to say, but then in a strange … but slow voice, he said that the library I had been in had been bombed by the Japanese when they took the island and that the woman was his former girlfriend and she had been killed when the library was totally demolished.

"Again, he looked at the photo he had and looked at me and said, did you really talk with her? I was almost in shock when I realised that for some strange reason, things just did not set right. If she had been killed, how could I have visited with her, talked with her and even enjoyed that ice-cold pineapple juice? The things she told me about the occupation of the Japanese was true so the pilot said, so I did not understand how it all took place, yet it did and when the other medic with me told him that he had seen my signature on the visitors log, I would swear I saw some tears form in the pilot's eyes as he looked at the black and white photo.

"We were supposed to land at Iowa Jima to refuel, but the pilot said we had plenty of fuel to make it to Japan, so he flew a circle around the island so we could all look out and see it from the air, then we continued on to Japan.

"It was an eight-hour trip in those old prop transporters, and we all tried to settle down and listen to some Japanese radio station over the radio. Time seemed to drag and suddenly, the pilot informed us that we were going to have to ditch because our fuel had gone so low and we could not make it as a headwind had hit us and we were in danger of running out of fuel!

"We did not have enough of those lifeboats you inflate on board, and they passed out the Mae West jackets for all of us to wear and he radioed to Japan to ask for standby when we ditched. We were all worried and I'm sure none of us knew how to swim in the ocean, but things were beginning to happen too fast for all of us to understand … for we were loaded with raw recruits who were to replace others in Japan.

"The captain came back and spoke with us, and told us how to inflate our Mae West jackets when we got into the water, and he showed us how to leave the aeroplane and said we had only five seconds to leave before the plane would sink beneath the water … then he turned and looked at me … for a very long time without saying anything, but I had an idea about what he was probably thinking.

"Time seemed to stand still and everyone was so silent that you could feel every bolt in the air transport rattle as we flew on towards Japan; and as I wondered about it, I wondered if any of us would make it for we were now flying over that dangerous Triangle between Guam and Japan.

"Some of the men prayed and others just looked with blank expressions, then I heard the voice of the librarian say: "Don't worry. You will make it." I looked around, but no one was there but the men who had come with us, and half an hour later I heard her say, "All is well."

"Then the pilot came and informed us we were over land and if we crashed the Mae West would be of no use. So he told us how to get out of the air transport once it struck the ground then he looked at me with a very sad face and for some reason, I smiled and said: "She said we would make it," and the captain seemed to feel better but no one else heard me.

"The captain then called over the intercom and said, to get ready for crash-landing, and as the minutes passed, we waited. We could feel the aircraft slowly going lower and as we looked out, we saw the airfield under us, and we landed, but as our wheels touched the runway, the motors all stopped together! We were out of fuel, and sitting in the middle of the airfield runway.

"We could hear the tower telling us to get the hell off the runway, but the captain who was the pilot, told him we had no fuel to go anywhere, so they sent a tractor to pull us back to the terminal where we all left the aeroplane; and as I was about to leave the captain walked over to me and said: "If you see her again, tell her I said: "THANKS" ... I thought he was going to crush my hand shaking it, then he said: "We ran out of fuel before we landed, but somehow we made it, but I think she was with us all the way." He then turned and walked away; and some of the other medics came up and asked me what the heck ... was as going on and why were we having to all walk back to the terminal tower. I could not explain and I guess I may never really know what happened.

"This actually took place in 1947 when I was shipped to Tokyo, Japan as a medical-surgical technician for the Far East Air Force; and was assigned to the 237th Medical Disp. In the Meiji Building on Avenue A in downtown Tokyo, Honshu, Japan.

"Through all these years I have wondered about the incident, but I have never seen or heard from the librarian, and I never did get to know the captain's last name. No way can I explain it all, let alone try to understand it."

A very interesting story. As a matter of interest, Leon Thompson later heard that they were going to replace the library that was demolished by the Japanese bombing.

You must agree ... I just had to include this story. I cannot explain it. It had to be a step back in time ... the Time Zone that we do not understand.

I can solve Victrola to which Leon Thompson made reference in his story ... According to Webster's Third New International Dictionary (Morocco bound as in the Crosby-Hope song), Victrola is trademark used for a phonograph. As stated, I just had to include this story due to the fact that every female who has typed it and proofed it has burst into tears.

Leon Thompson showing the epaulets of a Japanese Admiral that he brought back from Japan ... If it had been the Germany posting it might have been a few bars of the missing SS gold bars ... but that is another story.

'HI … I'M SID TWYNING …

*Sergeant Peter Hindley during his period with No.29 Squadron
(RAF Wattisham) seen here at Missile Practice Camp August
1970, at RAF Valley in Anglesey. Sergeant Hindley is second
from left on front row sitting on the Lightning wing.*

Let us follow the service career of Peter Hindley, for
although nothing further happened at RAF Leeming …
another strange incident was yet to unfold.

From RAF Leeming Junior Technician Hindley was
posted to RAF Geilenkirchen in Germany to No 3
Squadron who was equipped with English Electric
Canberra jet bombers. Their role was as a light-bomber
- night-intruder squadron.

In 1965 Hindley was posted back to England to RAF Watton in Norfolk. He was selected to work on the Special Installations Flight, which involved installing special electronic intelligence equipment into various aircraft. Hindley remained at RAF Watton for three years and, during that period at Watton, he was promoted to Sergeant. And, it was at RAF Watton where he had a very strange dream which, happened soon after his arrival at Watton in 1965, as he explains:

"I dreamed one night that I was standing in the middle of a virtually empty hangar, when a Sergeant came through the open hangar doors, walked straight up to me and said: 'Hi ... I'm Sid Twyning ... just posted in. Where's the Squadron Admin Office?' I directed him to it.

"I told my wife the following morning about the dream as the name was unusual and was so clear."

Sergeant Hindley thought no more about his dream and, it was put out of his mind. After his tour of duty at RAF Watton, he was posted to RAF Scampton in Lincolnshire; where he worked on the Blue Steel Missiles fitted to the Vulcan bombers.

In 1969 Sergeant Hindley was posted to RAF Wattisham in Suffolk, to No 29 Squadron who were equipped with the Lightning Jet Fighter; and it was his task to service the supersonic Lightnings.

In 1970 ... five years since his strange dream at RAF Watton ... an even stranger event was about to unfold as Peter Hindley recalls:

"One day I was standing in the hangar when I saw a Sergeant walking towards me. I somehow knew what he was going to say to me and sure enough he did. 'Hi … I'm Sid Twyning … just posted in. Where's the Squadron Admin Office?' … It was a most peculiar feeling."

What a strange dream … that came true five years later. Peter Hindley later told Sid Twyning what had happened and they became good friends.

Sergeant Peter Hindley came out of the RAF in 1973 after serving 15 years and at the time of the interview he lived in Warrington in Cheshire. And since his experiences whilst in the Royal Air Force he said:

"Since this experience I have been fascinated by deserted airfields and what tales they harbour."

Those old wartime; and in a strange sort of way – enchanting – silent airfields; that bring a tear or two, harbour many strange and eerie … chilling secrets; but none stranger than.

'Hi … I'm Sid Twyning …

THE LOCH NESS GHOST

Loch Ness, the home of Nessie the Monster and a ghost World War Two flier, is one of the largest freshwater lochs in Scotland.

'Loch Ness Monster is Nazi U-Boat' - screamed the full front-page of the Sunday Sport, Sunday, October 15, 1989. And, to support their claim, a photograph of a U-Boat that was said to have been taken two weeks earlier by an American tourist.

The German submarine was quickly linked to Rudolf Hess, the deputy Fuhrer and stories flowed like tales from the Arabian Nights; with as much credibility.

The German U-Boat in Loch Ness. This is Fiction. But what about the Loch Ness Monster; is that Fact or Fiction? And what about the Phantom Flier? How does the Phantom Second World War flier tie-in with Loch Ness and the Monster? Are they just stories created by people wanting publicity?

So, let us look at the facts that we have on record. Sightings of the Loch Ness Monster started in earnest during the 1930s and, one eye-witness account described the Monster as having a snake-like neck and head and was some fifty feet in overall length.

Over the years there have been many sightings, the sharp increase being due to the fact that communications across the Highlands of Scotland have improved, thus news of any sightings travels faster. Also, there is now a road by the loch-side. And, coupled with all that there is greater public awareness. Monster hunters have been out in force ... but no firm proof of Nessie.

One expert said the Loch Ness Monster is nothing more than mass-hallucination. And the noted anthropologist, Sir Arthur Keith, commented that the Loch Ness Monster was not a problem for zoologists but for psychologists.

But that is only their opinion. They do not have any proof to say that Nessie does **not** exist. The Monster Legend has been around a long-long- time; and goes back into the mists of time.

In AD550 Saint Adamnan wrote about the Life of Saint Columba and, in his work he vividly describes the rescue of the Pict named Lugne from the attack of a Monster in Loch Ness. At the sight of the Monster, Saint Columba made the sign of the Cross in front of it and commanded it in the name of God to return to the deep. The Monster slipped beneath the waters, to the utter amazement of the Picts; and from that moment on they were converted to Christianity.

Picts by the way, were people older than the Gaelic and Brythonic peoples who once occupied Britain and about the 9th century became finally amalgamated with the Scots ... bringing with them the Legend of the Loch Ness Monster.

So does the Loch Ness Monster exist? It does according to Hector Boece; who in 1527, recorded in his book Scotorum Historiae - the History of Scotland, an account of a terrible beast, as told by Duncan

Campbell who saw the Monster climb out of Loch Ness and kill three men.

So an eye-witness account and recorded. How many other sightings that, were **not** recorded. Remember, at this period, Loch Ness was very inaccessible and travel was very difficult, not like it is today.

Further evidence to support that a Monster was lurking in Loch Ness, came from the Duke of Portland who, wrote to The Times newspaper in the 1930's, to say that in 1895, the forester, local hotel keeper and fishing guides, spoke often of the Loch Ness Monster. So is there a Monster Sea Serpent?

"I was at the Loch early one morning, at the crack of dawn, camera at the ready;" said Pete Smithson, "Suddenly I saw this figure coming, weaving like, towards me. I thought he had been in some sort of accident. I then saw he was dressed in wartime flying clothes, complete with parachute and harness.

"As he sort of staggered towards me I suddenly felt cold. By now he was no more than 10 to 15 feet away and I could clearly see his RAF uniform. I shouted, 'Are you alright?' At that point he arched his right-hand and pointed towards the Loch.

"I instinctively turned and looked out over Loch Ness in the direction in which he was pointing. I fully expected to see the Monster. I then had a funny feeling … the coldness had gone and, quickly turning to the stranger shouted … 'what is it? But he had vanished. I then realized it had been a ghost airman. But he looked so real. The only thing about him was he looked injured and his face was greyish.

"What a damn fool I felt … confronted by a ghost … my camera around my neck, yet I never had an inkling to take a photo."

That sighting was in September 1978 and since then, two other people have also informed me that they had seen a figure of an airman near Loch Ness, which had vanished when near the Loch. They both said the figure had on parachute and harness.

So, what is the connection with the phantom airman? It is true that a Vickers twin-engined Wellington, N2980 R-Robert, crashed into Loch Ness on New Year's Eve, 1940. Caught in a snow storm one engine cut out and, unable to maintain height, the pilot, Squadron Leader Marwood-Elton, ordered the crew to bale out. They did so but the rear-gunner's parachute failed to open properly and he was killed. The Wellington bomber crashed in Loch Ness, the pilot and co-pilot having remained at the controls to keep the bomber steady while the crew made good their escape. They were unaware that the rear-gunner had been killed. Before the bomber sank into the Loch, they managed to scramble into the dinghy and, reach the safety of the shore.

So was it the air-gunner trying to give some sort of warning to the pilot? It is strange that the sightings of the Phantom World War Two flyer, only started in 1978; a year after Robin Holmes of Heriot-Watt University, Edinburgh; located the wartime bomber.

For 37 years Wellington N2980, R - Robert, had remained undisturbed. Now the bounty hunters were in full cry, for out of the 11,461 Wellingtons built, this was the only survivor. Yes, there had been hundreds, Germany had not destroyed them.

But after the war they were not wanted and melted down ... no one was interested ... now everybody was interested.

In September 1988 they started to lift R-Robert and all was going well when suddenly, something gave...the bomber sank back into the Loch. Was that a sign to call a stop...? Leave the Wellington bomber in peace... was that what the phantom flyer was trying to say...? Yes, without any shadow of doubt.

But they did not stop and after another attempt the Wellington bomber was brought out of the Loch...the tyres were still inflated and when a battery was put on, the navigation lights worked at once.

Today, Wellington N2980, R - Robert is at the Brooklands Museum being restored ... But what about the Phantom World War Two flyer? Is he at peace now his bomber has been removed from its last resting place? I think not. What do you think?

THE MISSING BUTTON

On reading the story about Bobby's Vigil in **Ghost Stations™** it prompted Sheila Staves to contact me regarding a strange experience that she had had in 1967. For 25 years she told no one, for fear that they would not believe her; but, on reading about Bobby and the other true stories in my **Ghost Stations™** she felt she just had to get it off her chest and tell someone, thankfully, it was to me and, I now have permission to publish her very interesting story.

In June 1967, Sheila Staves who now lives in Australia decided to visit RAF Ludford Magna in Lincolnshire, for sentimental reasons.

During those dark days of war, Sheila fell in love with one of those dashing aircrew in those hectic days. It had been a chance meeting and although only eighteen years old, Sheila was in love. This is her story; so I will let Sheila tell it in her own words:

"I first met Dixie Dean in October 1943 and I fell in love with him right from the start. It could have been because of the fuss he made over me … but I think it was more than that.

"He was very nice and, swept me off my feet. He said very little about what he did but I understood that he was a second pilot with the crew of Fraser Holland.

"I only saw him a few times but those times that we spent together will live with me forever. He wrote me a few letters in one said that he wanted to marry me as soon as he had completed his tour of operational missions which, he expected by the end of the year. So, I was looking forward to 1944.

"Ludford Magna was a terrible place and Dixie said it was always wet and cold. In one of his letters he said that he had lost a button from his tunic and if I found it, to keep it as a keepsake. I told him he had not lost it when with me and to ask his other girl friends. He said I was the only girl for him and that made me cry with happiness. I can still see him now.

"That was the last I saw of him and it was not until many weeks later did I learn that his Lancaster bomber, 'O' for Orange, had been shot down over Germany in early December.

"I cried. It was very hard for Dixie had been my first love and only love. After the war I got married but still had thoughts of Dixie, hence my visit to Ludford Magna in 1967. At that time I had been married twenty years and suddenly had an urge to visit RAF Ludford Magna. I had never seen it since the war years, then for only once.

"It was a nice warm day and I parked my car on a concrete lay-by that looked as if it had been part of the airfield. It all looked so different. It all seemed so peaceful and strange.

"I had a picnic basket with me and I sat down on the grass at the side of the hard-standing. I had asked a local man who was working nearby if it was all right to be there and it was he who said the concrete sections were where the bombers used to be parked.

"It was so lovely and peaceful and I must admit, a few tears fell as I thought back to those dark days of war but, for me, were very happy days. I must have dozed off for I felt that Dixie was there with me and, that lost button he had found and was going to give it to me. I was brought back to earth with a shout ... 'Lady, are you alright?' ... shouted the man to whom I had spoken earlier. I replied that I was and as I put the things back into my picnic basket ... I noticed something at the edge of my car rug in some concrete rubble. I moved the dirt and picked up an RAF button.

"I cried. It was the lost button. I believe I was destined to find it," she said. "For me, that is Dixie's lost button."

That is the story behind the missing button, found by Sheila Staves in some concrete rubble at the side of a hard-standing. To her, it is her lover's lost button. It was obviously from an RAF Best Blue uniform; so could well have been someone courting there on a sunny day and had a loose button – very easy for it to come off on that type of button if loose.

It is a fact that Sheila Staves was meant to find it and to her ... it is her sweet-heat's lost button.

THE GRINDON GHOSTS

*The haunted Cavalier Inn at Grindon and home for the
Grindon Ghosts*

Grindon is a remote moor-land village in the Peak
National Park and due to its height above sea level (800
feet) is frequently covered by low clouds and mist. In
the severe 1947 winter it was cut off from the outside
world by snow. In February 1947, Halifax RT922
crashed on Grindon Moor in Staffordshire, some eight
miles east of Leek, whilst dropping hay in snow for
stranded animals. All onboard, including a number of
pressmen were killed. A memorial window was erected
in Grindon Church and pieces of the wreckage can be
found on a display board in The Cavalier Inn located in
the centre of the village.

The Inn is an old building erected in the late 17th century and has been a public house for over 100 years. Formerly called the Shoulder of Mutton … probably when sheep drovers stopped while en route to market, the Inn was renamed the Cavalier by a previous owner some 30 years ago. In February 1988, Bob Blunden purchased the Inn and, it was not long before he began to hear about the alleged hauntings. The locals told of a grey haired man dressed in grey that would walk down the stairs from the private accommodation.

"Initially we treated the stories with some cynicism until we began to note various occurrences," said Bob Blunden. "Glasses would move off the shelves and crash to the floor. One Thursday evening, a sherry barrel on a shelf behind the bar, was lifted above the surrounding bottles and similarly crashed to the floor. This was witnessed by several customers. We also discovered that one of the reasons the previous owners sold was because the wife was scared of the ghost.

"On other days there would be a smell at the end of the bar; akin to rotting compost … which I could smell but my wife could not. Similarly, when resting upstairs in the private lounge, my wife frequently complained about a horrible smell, and from her description it was the same as the smell that I experienced in the bar.

"On many occasions as we closed up for the night we heard a small child's voice come from the dining room saying "nite, nite" and we both felt a presence on the stairs of a small animal. Frequently the heavy inner door to the main bar would open and close … yet nobody entered the pub. One Bank Holiday, we were talking to some customers about our experiences; and they decided not to tell us that their daughter, who was allegedly psychic, was visiting them the following day.

"The following day I noted the customers talking to their daughter, all sitting on an old leather settle in the dining room; when suddenly, a suit of armour at the end of the dining room fell over with a loud crash. The daughter said that she saw a little boy push it ... yet there was nobody else in the dining room.

"Glasses continued to crash to the floor ... and a pint mug would suddenly start to swing like mad on the hooks above the bar. In addition, the beer would mysteriously switch off in the cellar. Then one night after we had retired we awoke to my son screaming. On climbing up to his bedroom in the attic; he was screaming 'keep her away from me.'

"We comforted him and told him he was dreaming, but further investigation revealed that Roy Shenton, a previous barman at the pub, had slept in the same room and had experienced visitations from a woman with long grey hair dressed in a long black dress. He said that she used to sit on the end of his bed and he used to pull the covers over his head hoping that she would go away. Eventually he ended up having medical treatment, as his nerves got so bad.

"The smells and disturbances continued until we left the pub in June 1990. As far as I am aware they continue to this day."

BLOTTING OUT THE PAST

"Having just obtained the three **Ghost Stations™** books, it is Hornchurch and North Weald entries which prompted me to contact you," said Desmond Keen.

And Desmond's information may help many of my Readers understand why the old airfields have a 'tear on the wind', as their heroic past was sadly blotted out.

Desmond Keen continues: "As a mere National Service shorthand-typist, my first posting was to the Aviation Candidates Selection Boards at RAF Hornchurch in October 1946.

"I had previously been stationed at Euston House in London, it was here only a lodger unit housed in the central hangar, which always seemed like a great empty cathedral to me. All one could see from the office windows on those late winter afternoons was the grim approach of the evening mists over the deserted airfield; no one ever spoke to us of the wartime glories of the place.

"The iron hand of authority seemed anxious to blot out the station's battle experiences and return everything to pre-war RAF standards.

"I remember seeing the last of the aircrew wall-painting being obliterated from the old barrack blocks on the square soon after I got there.

"The ACSB staff lamented the loss of their convenient spot in London and morale was poor - especially as we suffered the 1947 winter there. The unit was moved to North Weald in April 1947 - reasons unknown - and then, to our dismay, we had to return to Hornchurch in October 1948.

"By then the name had been changed to the Combined Selection Centre - CSC and, it is at this point I was puzzled by the entry in Book One (page 154) which refers to a large rambling building on the edge of the airfield. It had formerly been used as the Officers' Mess.

"We understood that it was the sergeants who had all been evicted from their fine modem premises - much bad feeling - in order to provide us with offices and interview rooms, as the work had grown and the hangar offices were inadequate.

"I remained there until March 1949 and once again for me and my friends, it was an unhappy place."

And because they squashed the memories of those gallant airmen ... they return ... like the Ghost of Montrose and many, many others ... to haunt the old airfields.

THE GHOSTS OF THE WHITE LODGE INN

Mrs Melita Gibson in the haunted restaurant at the White Lodge Inn

In the spring of 1987 Colin and Melita Gibson bought the Greig Manor Hotel at Risca in South Wales. The restaurant was quite rundown, and at the suggestion of Melita's father, Denny Densham, they renamed it … The White Lodge Inn and Restaurant.

Over the past few months they have worked very hard and steadily built up the business. Since then several strange incidents have taken place; and one of the most unusual took place in one of the restaurant rooms. A group were enjoying a very pleasant meal, when quite suddenly, a glass candle holder lifted into the air and plunged to the floor.

The guests were startled by the incident and, about eight people witnessed it. No one could offer an explanation for the strange occurrence. "Must be haunted," someone said.

Very possibly so. And it seems that all the spirits in the bar are not all in the bottles, for on Christmas Day, 1987; one of the glasses floated up and crashed on to the floor. On New Years Day another glass took to the air, then crashed to the floor … this time, six people witnessed … in awe …the floating glass and one of them claimed that he saw a woman dressed in Victorian clothes; leave the bar just after the glass crashed onto the floor.

Since the floating glasses there have been many other strange events … one of the Bar Ladies saw, on two occasions, an old lady … dressed in what looked like a Victorian costume, walk out of the bar. And a very puzzling mystery is the bottles of spirits that have been removed from the optics and somehow placed on the top of the bar, without a drop being spilled. A guest, who spent the night at The White Lodge Inn, heard somebody walking about on the landing and went to investigate; but no one was there. So it does appear that the new owners have inherited a ghost or ghosts.

The resident ghosts seem quite friendly and helpful as the owner found out first hand. He had been working very hard throughout the day and was ready for a sit down and a bite to eat. He made himself comfy in front of the television but in a short time he fell fast asleep. The central heating had switched off and the room soon began to get chilly. Suddenly he felt a hand on his shoulder … shaking him awake. "Something told me to go to bed," he said. "The television was still on but issuing the high frequency whistle tone." Still half asleep he made his way to bed; and it was only after a good sleep, did he realise that he was quite alone the pervious night ... So who shook him on the shoulder?

A medium that visited The White Lodge Inn said he could sense two ghosts. A pipe smoking old man and an old lady. That would account for the strong smell of pipe smoke that Denny Densham could smell as he sat in the room watching television; but what about all the other sightings … and why the broken glasses?

Also, why was it that Denny did not see the ghosts? I asked him if he had ever seen a ghost.

"Yes," he replied, "I have seen two ghosts. One was in wartime at Barnes, it was a solid figure of a man dressed in a Dickensian outfit with cloak and top hat, which, was standing directly in my path as I walked along the pavement to get my bus. It was so solid I said; 'Oh sorry' as I did a little skip jump around him so as not to bump into him. When I looked back he had vanished. This only happened once and I have no explanation for it.

"Some years later when commercial television was about to start, I went into a partnership with two others and, converted part of an old Victorian Barnet Ensign photographic plate factory, into a small compact film studio. We were the first people in a new little industrial estate to get the phone connected and, so, from time to time, newcomers would come across to borrow our phone. Unfortunately, some abused the privilege and began to sneak in and make long distance calls without paying. Because of this we nailed up our back entrance, which, was located beside my office. There was a glass window in the wall overlooking the passage from this door. One afternoon my secretary, our studio electrician and myself, were having tea in this office, when a workman in overalls clumped down this passage from outside. We all saw him pass the window and I immediately picked up the telephone to warn my partner who had his office by the front door, telling him to stop this man, as he had no right to be in the building.

"We never found him; he had vanished just like my Dickensian man. Most amazing, was that just a week before we had laid a heavy duty lino in that passage; and found that we could not repeat the sound of his footsteps, because the lino muffled them. Despite a search through the local newspaper files, going back over 100 years, we could not find a story which might have linked the building with some death or tragedy."

It is very strange that Denny Densham described the ghost he saw as dressed in a Dickensian outfit and, the ghost in the bar being dressed in Victorian clothes, for there were three or more sightings of a ghost at RAF Llandon, South Glamorgan, during 1943 and 1945; and those who saw the ghost said it was dressed in old fashioned clothes. It was here they melted down those faithful Lancaster bombers ... and many times a ghostly figure in a stove-pipe hat was watching over them.

"He sort of resented what we were doing," said one airman.

It was a tragedy not to save some of those faithful bombers and, from the hundreds of pilots taught to fly at Llandon, many failed to return and, were killed in action ... that is also a tragedy.

But why does there have to be a tragedy to find a ghost? That is certainly not the case with the Ghosts of

The White Lodge Inn. Research shows that the building was originally a hunting lodge and is over a hundred years old. So, it is quite possible that many real-life strange happenings took place there.

Whatever did take place, had to have a good side to it for the ghosts seem to remain friendly for the place has a very, very peaceful atmosphere, despite the psychic happenings … drop in and see when next in the Risca area; and buy a friendly Spirit a drink.

The White Lodge Inn and Restaurant at Risca, South Wales where several strange incidents have taken place.

THE SUITCASE GHOST

The headquarters of the Kingston ATC Squadron is haunted by the suitcase ghost ... so it is alleged.

Many people have reported hearing heavy footsteps; very strange, for the floor is carpeted.

So it has to be haunted? If so, by whom? The answer must come from a certain suitcase, for when ever anyone looks into the suitcase; the ghostly footsteps are heard, as if resenting the intrusion into the suitcase.

So what is inside the suitcase? Inside the suitcase is a Royal Flying Corps uniform that is said to have belonged to Captain James McCudden ... who won the Victoria Cross in the First World War and, was mysteriously killed ... just like Lt. Arthur at Montrose.

McCudden was one of the greatest airmen of both the First World War and the Second World War.

He was in a class of his own. James McCudden was born on March 28, 1895, at Gillingham, Kent. He joined the Royal Flying Corps as a mechanic in May 1913. In January 1916, he was awarded the Croix de Guerre and, in September of the same year, the Military Medal. He got his commission in January 1917.

The following month McCudden won the Military Cross ... with a Bar in October of the same year. The Distinguished Service Order came in December 1917, with a Bar in January 1918.

In April 1918, he was awarded the Victoria Cross and, the citation read:

'For most conspicuous bravery, exceptional perseverance, keenness and a very high devotion to duty. Captain McCudden has at the present time accounted for 54 enemy aeroplanes.'

In July 1918, James McCudden was promoted Temporary Major and killed at Marquiz on leaving to take over his new squadron; the last thing he had told his batman was … "look after my new uniform in my suitcase."

McCudden was flying on ahead but he never made it. His aircraft crashed in mysterious circumstances. It was not an enemy aeroplane that brought him down; and it was not an enemy aircraft that brought down Lieutenant Arthur's aeroplane; and that mysterious accident brought about the Ghost of Montrose Aerodrome – See **Ghost Stations™2**.

"Look after my new uniform," he told his batman.

So beware if you touch the RFC uniform in the suitcase at the HQ of the Kingston ATC Squadron.

If you do, you will incur the wrath of Captain James McCudden, for that RFC uniform is surely his.

The ghostly footsteps are there to warn you to stay away from the suitcase.

Take heed.

BORLEY CHURCH & BORLEY RECTORY

On the borders of the counties of Essex and Suffolk near Long Melford, just north of Sudbury on the main A134 road, is the site of the most haunted house in England; that being Borley Rectory. And, since the Reverend H.D. Bull built it in 1863, it has been plagued with psychic happenings, which have been witnessed and experienced, by more people than any other alleged haunted house, anywhere in the world.

And, since I made reference in my previous book, to the fact that Borley was the most haunted site in the world, letters poured in to know more about the ghostly happenings at Borley. So let us delve into the spooky history of Borley Church and Borley Rectory … the Stars of the Spirit World.

With such a haunting reputation, Borley Rectory attracted the interest of many professional ghost hunters; one being Harry Price, a highly respected paranormal researcher – many say not so. Price turned his full attention on Borley Rectory and set up a thorough investigation into the paranormal happenings … witnessing many of the phenomena himself.

As a haunted house, Borley Rectory had everything including a colony of bats. Those little creepy devils flapping around the eerie night sky only enhanced Borley Rectory's reputation in the Spirit World. It was a gaunt Victorian building that had been added to from time to time. Everyone who lived in the house – and literally hundreds of visitors – all claimed that they had felt … heard … or saw things which could not have been explained by normal means. The catalogue of strange events is so varied it covers almost the entire field of psychic happenings. They include the movement and sometimes materialization and disappearance of objects … the ringing of bells, despite the fact that the wires had been cut, the opening and closing of locked doors, inexplicable noises, unearthly sighs and moans and odours … sometimes pleasant, sometimes decidedly unpleasant … like the smell of decaying corpses.

And many people claim to have seen a phantom coach and horses near the haunted house. Probably the most famous ghost of all is the Borley Nun, which is said to manifest itself during a full moon. Strangely enough the destruction of Borley Rectory was predicted in a séance and, in February 1939, the haunted rectory was completely gutted by fire that seem to start spontaneously while the building was unoccupied. It was all so very strange and mysterious.

After the fire Harry Price continued his ghost busting investigation. He excavated the cellars and here he unearthed part of the skull of a woman. Assuming this belonged to the ghostly nun he gave it a Christian burial at Liston Churchyard. Everyone now assumed that peace would reign over the troubled site … but did it?

The skull was laid to rest … but not the troubled spirits. They continued to roam unabated around the old rectory site. The Christian burial had not lain to rest the supernatural happenings. Borley was obviously the site of deep-rooted occult phenomena.

Many people still believed the site was haunted, two such people being Geoffrey Croom-Hollingsworth and Roy Potter. In March 1970 they set out to investigate the continued psychic happenings at the site of the rectory and, also at Borley Church, which, is reputedly, the most haunted church in England.

As dedicated, down to earth people, they spent hours and hours on the project, often during freezing weather conditions. They delved deeply into the biographies of the people who originally lived at Borley Rectory. They were particularly interested in members of the Bull family; and their research showed that previous biographers had not been very accurate with their facts. The Bull family had not been delved into properly and they had a key role to play, having witnessed manifestations. They had featured so strongly at Borley therefore, the facts had to be put right.

Over the next few months dozen of people were interviewed throughout the country; and it was back-breaking work with very little reward. Then came a lucky break. By sheer fluke, they bought a diary written by the eldest Bull girl, Caroline Sarah Elizabeth Bull. And of all the Bull girls, she was the only one that married. She wrote the diary when she was 21-years-of-age. The diary showed that in 1885, Borley Rectory was a very, very happy place. Although, it was clear that Reverend Bull knew all about the spectral nun; and, used to sit many hours in the summer-house by the lawn – in fact he erected the summer house – to watch the spectral nun swaying gently along the wall.

Caroline Bull wrote in her diary about many psychic happenings, the most detailed being about moving chairs. From her writings it was clear she was not afraid. Everybody interviewed said the Bull family was not a strange family. They were a Victorian family with Victorian values and, what they said could be taken as absolute gospel truth. They were very down to earth people; not publicity seekers.

Today the villagers are resistant to talk about the psychic happenings at Borley and this is quite understandable. The publicity that followed Harry Price's ghost busting investigation drew crowds of tourists into the area. Unfortunately, some of those people misbehaved quite badly causing damage to property and making life difficult for the residents.

The Ghost Busters did get results and, some rewarding eye-witness reports. One man travelling home one night had a terrifying experience. He was travelling on a motorbike along the road and, as he neared Borley he saw to his amazement, a coach coming across the field, across the road and into Borley Rectory. A phantom coach and horses driven by a phantom coachman … Unable to stop, the terrified motorcyclist passed right through the phantom coach. "It was an eerie, cold sensation," he said.

But this experience was not unique for during the Second World War a soldier had an identical encounter. An army despatch rider, who knew nothing about

Borley being haunted was coming up the hill towards Borley Church, the rectory on the left and the church on the right; when to his amazement ... he saw the phantom coach coming across the field. It passed right in front of him and ... he also was unable to stop and passed right through the phantom coach. It was all over in seconds but it left a vivid impression on the young military despatch-rider. He told only his wife for fear of being called an idiot; and when she laughed at him he did a bit of investigation to find out if the area was haunted. He was well aware of what he had seen, a phantom coach and horses ... very, very clearly. The despatch rider spent his next leave asking around the village; and was told that what he had seen was the phantom coach coming along the old River Road. Always when a full moon ... the phantom coach can be seen along the old River Road; but beware they warned him. With that warning the army despatch-rider decided enough was enough.

Roy Potter and Geoffrey Croom-Hollingsworth experienced a wealth of psychic events for which they had no rational explanation. These included ... ghostly footsteps on the road outside the church; but no one was there. Yet, the footsteps were very clear. And poltergeist activity in the porch can be attributed to the fact that the spirit did not want to be recorded.

An expensive tape recorder was set up in the porch of Borley Church and left running unattended. After only a few minutes there was a loud crash in the porch. This startled the two volunteers who were keeping watch on the church and they were so frightened, they dare not go forward to see what had happened. Instead they asked for help via their walkie-talkies.

Roy and Geoffrey raced to their assistance, not knowing what to expect and the first at the church porch was Geoffrey, who said: "To our dismay and horror, on the porch floor, which is stone, worse luck for us, was our tape recorder which was pretty well battered and all the tape had come off the reels and all over the place."

Borley Rectory in the time of the Bull family. The Bull girls seen happily playing on the lawn.

Since the demolition of Borley Rectory an orchard has been planted on the site but, this does not seem to have removed the cause of the hauntings for many ghostly sounds have been heard in the orchard; including raps ... the panting of a dog ... the sound of smashing crockery ... and sounds of heavy furniture being moved about. It was in the haunted orchard where the Ghost Busters had a very odd supernatural experience; as Geoffrey Croom-Hollingsworth explains:

"Here again, it was moonlight and the funny thing is, the time when most paranormal things happen at Borley, it has been a full moon. It was a full moon again tonight. This time we were in the garden of the bungalow. There is a small hedge, which runs along by the side of the bungalow that separates the ground of the bungalow from where the rectory was.

"We were stood there; very, very quite. When all of a sudden ... we heard this thudding in the rectory grounds. It was a kind of thud ... thud ... thud. It was a most peculiar sound, which we could not account for at all. And then we saw the fruit trees, which, are growing where the rectory actually stood. The branches of the fruit trees, moved. Yet there was no wind at all ... it was absolutely still.

"The most remarkable thing of this was that something came to the fence and gave it an almighty clunk. And that is the only time I have seen my colleague Roy, step back."

At first they thought it might be some animal so they threw stones in the vicinity of the sound, just in case it was an animal and would scare it away. But it did not stop the paranormal force. "As it came towards the tree … the tree seemed to shake about a bit," said Roy. "So we looked down to see if anything was down there and we saw nothing. Then there was this great big bang on the fence and that was when I stepped back, thinking; was it an animal, was something going to come over … yet we saw nothing at all."

On another occasion, just a week after the tape recorder incident; the Ghost Busters were back at Borley. It was very misty conditions and all was very quiet. Suddenly at about 0300 hours they heard talking and laughter; men's and girl's voices. They thought that people were walking along the road so they made their way over to the direction of the voices; which carried very clearly on the still early morning air, but when they got to the road … no one was there. A chill came over the Ghost Busters. "When I walked toward the hedge, bordering the road, the voices seemed to be concentrating on the hedge … just like coming along," said Croom-Hollingsworth.

The voices just carried on and on; very, very clear. So clear they thought there had to be people. Sound travels at night. So Roy got into the car and coasted - he did not start the engine - down the hill.

He stayed down there and with his walkie-talkie sent back the following message: "Nobody down here whatsoever - There is nobody along the Melford Road."

So far the Ghost Busters had drawn a blank. Yes, they had experienced many strange paranormal happenings, which they could not explain; but, they had not seen any ghosts especially the Borley Nun that, they hoped would manifest itself to them. But it did do so for over twelve minutes, as Geoffrey Croom-Hollingsworth explains:

"I was stood in the rectory garden. I looked down the garden and I could definitely see it was someone with a cowl and habit. All of a sudden this figure seemed to glide across their garden. I was still rather sceptical until it came to the hedge that borders their garden and then it went through there without making any noise whatsoever. At this stage I contacted Roy and told him to get over to me quick. The figure then went into the garage then came within twelve feet of me and I was then able to observe the figure properly.

"I could clearly see it was a nun in a habit. The habit was grey. The face, from what I could see, wasn't of a young person, more of a woman in her sixties. The nun then went through the hedge again. By this time Roy had arrived and we both followed her about twelve feet behind. When the ghostly nun came to the ditch, there was no water in it, there was a plank by means of getting across; she went across there just as though the whole thing was filled in … yet it was a very wide ditch.

"We followed, crossing the ditch by means of the plank and we saw the nun disappear through a pile of bricks that was stacked up in the garden. That was the last we saw of the ghost."

Neither of the Ghost Busters were frightened at the sight of the ghost. "I don't think there is anything to be afraid of," said Geoffrey. "In this instance … I didn't feel any animosity. It was a very close sensation; it was peaceful … it was tranquil."

Did it actually happen? Had the Ghost Busters managed to raise a ghost and witnessed the manifestation of the Borley Nun? Raising a Spirit was one of the occult feats claimed by John Dee 1527-1608 the most celebrated English psychic experimenter of the 16th century. A skilled politician, Dee was an adviser to Queen Elizabeth the First; and a very respected man, as so Geoffrey Croom-Hollingsworth. But to find out for himself, Denny Densham decided to investigate the claims made and join them on their next visit to Borley.

Denny Densham was not the kind of man who could be tricked. During the Second World War he was a Front-Line War Correspondent and arrived in Normandy ten days after D-Day, 6 June 1944, to cover the Allies push into Europe. Death and destruction lay all around him and he covered it all on film.

"Very extraordinary times," he said. Always a man to be in first; and he was happy to join the Ghost Busters Team. So, with Denny at the helm we follow their progress in the hunt for a ghost or two.

They selected Borley Church for their first investigation and arrived at midnight; not for any special paranormal reason, but to off set the chance of anyone else in the area that might disturb them.

Their first task was to search the church thoroughly. And, as soon as they were satisfied the church was empty; they placed a cassette near the Altar. Then two of the team took up station in a pew at the opposite end of the church; and instructed the other members of the team to lock them in. "It was an eerie experience," said Denny, "and there were certainly some odd sounds generated … including loud and small raps."

I have the master tape of the Borley Church investigation; and one can clearly hear the raps that Denny refers to. They are a very ghostly sound … rap … rap … rap.

They heard and recorded many strange things; a sort of bump sound originating near the Altar. this was picked up by the recorder at the end of the church … clunk … bump … it was very strange and spine chilling. No member of the Ghost Busters Team was responsible…that was for certain; for it was not a time for jokes.

Intrigued, they then locked two tape recorders in the church. One by the Altar and the other at the opposite end by the main door. The Ghost Busters then sealed the church and kept a watch outside for the next thirty minutes.

"During this period the ghost decided to make its presence known; and to our utter astonishment we recorded the sound of it opening a door," said Denny. And he added: "This was not only eerie but stranger still … because the door did not exist. It is interesting to note; that the recorder placed near the main door picked up the sound as well but at a much fainter level."

So the team had a pretty good idea where it had originated. It was obvious the noise could not have come from the main door of the church. So, they immediately paid attention to the only other door into the church ... the chancel door.

The haunted Borley Church and church yard ... the scene of many strange paranormal happenings.

On investigation ... the door had a curtain over it and was securely bolted. They tried the bolt to see what sort of sound it made ... it did not squeak.

That brought to an end the ghost hunt and Denny Densham had been impressed with what he had seen and heard; so much so, his opinion of the Borley haunting had changed considerably, as had all the team and they decided to return the following week.

They returned a week later and entered the church at about thirty minutes past midnight; and the atmosphere within seemed quite normal. So normal in fact that they all remarked about it. The first half-hour recording proved to be negative.

For the second session they set up a semi-professional tape recorder with two high quality microphones; one of which, was placed near the Altar and the other about half way down the isle in the centre of the church. And in addition, a cassette machine was also set up by the Altar, as a back up.

Having thoroughly searched the church to make sure it was completely empty, they started the machines running and locked them in. As they did so, they felt a sudden change in the atmosphere and one of the team said: "I have a feeling we are begin watched."

This session proved to be very interesting, in more ways than one. After a few minutes the microphone placed in the centre of the church picked up a clatter as though some object had been thrown down near it. For some reason, which the Ghost Busters cannot explain, a considerable amount of static seemed to be generated … just before and during the sound … clang … a few minutes later began to pick up static again … then came faint sounds of something moving about in the vicinity of the Altar. Then they heard one sound that was quite unexpected. "It sent a chill through our marrows, for the microphone, in the centre of the church had picked up quite clearly, what obviously is a human sigh," said Denny.

During the next recording session the cassette recorder jammed completely; and very mysteriously, the tape was pulled out and strewn all over the Altar.

"It seemed as though this was an indication that our presence was resented," said Denny. As they feared that damage might occur to the tape machine; they packed it away and left a replacement cassette machine, by the Altar. This was not a top quality machine for it tended to pick up the sound of its own motors running. Nevertheless, it recorded some very strange psychic sounds.

First of all there was a sort of whirring noise … a fluttering. The Ghost Busters Team thought this noise might have been made by some animal; and at the time Denny said: "There didn't seem to be any other explanation for it." But that theory was soon to be ruled out; for at about 03:45 hours they recorded the sound of a door being opened again … although this sound was similar to the previous one … it lacked the squeak of the bolt. Then silence prevailed as the spirits melted back into the dark unknown.

As dawn approached the Ghost Busters packed up their equipment; and after discussion of events so far, they decided to break the sequence of visits and try again during the summer months, for although they could not find any reason for the ghostly sounds, they wanted to check and see if the warm dry conditions had any effect on the paranormal happenings.

For security reasons, for the Borley Ghosts had now attracted so much interest they kept the date of their visit a secret. And, as an additional safeguard, they changed they minds a couple of times. Finally, they set off in July. It was a very dark evening but warm enough for them not to wear top coats.

The Ghost Busters Team, again with Denny Densham, started recording at 0100 hours and the tapes revealed only the natural pervading atmosphere of the church and nothing else. "There was not a single click or rap audible," said Denny. "But, as we entered the church at 0145 hours we all felt a change in the atmosphere." And he added: "It is hard to describe the sensations some of us felt; tingles running through our bodies. Others claimed they felt there was a presence in the church. It was all very eerie and strange."

From such an unearthly feeling, the Ghost Busters just knew the next session would produce a result … and it did do … their feelings had been justified.

It started with the sound of movements somewhere near the Altar. This was followed by the sound of a door shutting; But once again, a door that does not exist … clunk … bang. There was about ten minutes silence; only the natural ambience of the church and the cassette motor. Then came a crash as if something had been knocked over. At that point the team became aware of the increase in the background noise on the tape. Then another strange sound occurred … it ended with a sort of pop. This was followed by a much louder … pop or explosion … then minutes later; an unearthly sound that sent shivers through the Ghost Busters. "It was the sort of effect one imagines haunted houses to produce," said Denny.

It originated just in front of the Altar Rail; the sound of heavy footsteps on a wooden floor, yet the floor in front of the Altar is of stone ... clunk ... clunk ... clunk ... clunk ... then the sound of someone or something moving a heavy object across a wooden floor; followed by the sound of heavy footsteps, clunk ... clunk ... clunk. Footsteps as if someone was walking away; but sounded as if on a **wooden** floor. "If those were footsteps; they must have belonged to a very large and powerful man," said Denny. Eight minutes later there was another sound generated; but none of the Ghost Busters had any ideas what it represented. It sounded like moving books or papers ... an eerie clattering.

The Ghost Busters Team, with Denny Densham included, returned to Borley Church the following August and during the small hours of the morning, they all observed a glow around the chancel door. As though a phosphorescent aura was being generated. It was an occult phenomena being generated around the chancel door ... the Devil inviting the Ghost Busters into the church. The phosphorescent aura magnetized all of them, including Denny Densham, who said: "It was clearly witnessed by all of the team ... it was not a photism ... it was not imaginary ... it was real.

On this particular night, the ghost made its presence known by producing some more sounds; which ended with a very frightening moaning sigh ... a sound of footsteps … clunk … clunk; like the dull thumping sound of footsteps walking on a wooden floor, then a long pause, sound of a heavy object being moved, then a deep sigh or like a dog or similar animal coughing.

For their fifth visit to Borley the Ghost Busters decided to man the church throughout the entire night. "On previous occasions we seemed to get the best results by leaving the equipment locked in the empty building … we thought perhaps the human presence had some adverse effect on conditions," said Denny Densham.

Three of the Ghost Busters Team kept watch from the choir stalls adjacent to the Altar and settled down on their ghost watch; and it proved to be a memorable and frightening occasion.

Once again the church became very cold; as if a forewarning, despite the fact it was a warm summer night. There were numerous clicks … and raps … from the vicinity of the font. And one time they heard a sound as though heavy timbers were being crushed. But in the darkness they could not see what was happening. Then, at 0430 hours they began to observe tiny points of light hovering in the curtain behind the font. As they looked on in amazement; more tiny lights appeared on one of the pews about a quarter of the way down the church. "At first we thought we couldn't believe our own eyes," said Denny. "And we broke the silence to speak about it." One of the team said: "I must be getting tired for I keep seeing things." Almost at the same time Geoffrey said: "Look at the curtains." Denny replied by saying: "Look at the first few pews." "In the curtain … on the right hand side," shouted one of the team excitedly. The atmosphere inside the haunted church was electrifiable. "Like fireflies", said Denny. "Yes." … But what did it all mean. The tiny lights were not fireflies. So, what did it all mean? It was certainly not imagination; and the tiny lights had to be connected with an occult phenomenon. Three of the Ghost Busters Team could clearly see the tiny lights. After a few minutes … during which time the tiny lights had increased their numbers; they suddenly began to move towards the Ghost Busters. This made them very fearful at the sudden change of events. They were locked inside the church and they knew that there were no other human beings inside the church with them. They were alone … except for the Forces of Evil.

But were they the Forces of Evil? Or were they Paranormal Forces protecting their Spectral World? As the ghostly lights moved slowly towards them they changed into long strips of light … a spell-binding phenomenon that mesmerised the Ghost Busters.

"It was then something threw an object at us," said Denny. "That was very unnerving and it made all the team jump. All the time it was getting colder and colder … like a build-up of power. The top of my head had gone very cold and if I had had hair on my head it would have been standing on end."

By this time it had turned extremely cold inside the haunted church and all the team wanted to do was to get out. Released from the haunted church, the Ghost

Busters gathered themselves together; and almost immediately made a painstaking and through search of the church, but they could find nothing to account for the incident. Can one explain the unnatural forces? Supernatural forces that are beyond the scientifically known or recognizable phenomena, which are found in and around Borley Church and on the site of the Old Borley Rectory. "There doesn't seem to be any evidence that whatever produced those sounds was trying to communicate directly with us," said Denny Densham.

It could be argued that throwing that object and, the violent attack on the tape recorder left in the porch, was a warning that perhaps somebody or something resented the presence of the Ghost Busters.

But it was not just the Spirits who resented the Ghost Busters the locals do also. A few years ago the BBC did a programme about the hauntings at Borley Church, for it was an amazing investigation. The programme fired the imagination of hundreds of people and ghost-hunters flocked in their dozens to Borley Church. But they created havoc for the local residents and police were needed to patrol the area. They moved on anyone hovering in the vicinity of Borley Church. And, for that reason Borley Church is now locked at night and the authorities have banned any future psychic investigations. But is that the real reason? Or is there a much deeper and sinister reason for keeping out the ghost hunters and serious psychic researchers? Has the Pagan Church made a pact with the Devil?

Many Pagan cults were never erased during the growth of major religions such as Christianity. They have remained dormant; awaiting the right time to surface. With the church in extreme rapid decline. Is now the right time? It was only the church that, from about the fourteenth century, started to condemn the Occult practices as evil.

And, it was not Christianity that changed healing from an occult art into a science ... it was Hippocrates (460 - 377 B.C.), teaching that illness was due to natural causes and curable by natural means. What the church could not understand ... it condemned as Evil.

Man has always felt ... and always will ...the presence of hidden forces around him. The Albigenses sect of heretics living in the south of France; held the belief that the material world was created by the Devil.

However, one thing that is certain; despite numerous Exorcism attempts, Séances and the Christian burial of that skull fragment ... something Supernatural and connected with Occult phenomena remains in Borley Church. As one enters the haunted Borley Church one can hardly fail to notice a certain cold...eerie Supernatural feeling in the atmosphere. A chilling welcome to the most haunted Church in England.

And, although Borley Rectory is no longer there, the surrounding area can still be called ... the most haunted site in the world.

THE HAUNTED CHURCH – THE FACTS

Another view of Borley Church seen in beautiful sunlight... but a much different atmosphere at night.

The File The Most Haunted Church, in the original **Ghost Stations™** created a lot of interest. It covered Borley Church and Borley Rectory.

I used material from the master tape of the Borley investigation, which was a serious investigation by serious minded people. As you now know, I hold the master tape and an audio tape, of An Investigation Into The Haunting of Borley Church.

Following an excellent review in the Psychic News, it brought forth a letter from a Doctor Louis Mayerling who said that Borley Rectory was not haunted. I replied in very strong terms to put the record straight; and, standby what I had written about Borley Church and Rectory in my **Ghost Stations™** that being the recordings made in the church are a 100 per cent genuine. I have looked through my Borley Rectory files so let us go over a few of the facts and, include a few that I might have missed; you, the Reader, can then make up your own mind. To support the following facts, you must also have read the previous story.

Borley Rectory, from day one, has always been a cold building, never a home, always a building. It was said to be haunted from day one; however, the eldest Bull girl's diary showed that in 1885, Borley Rectory was a very happy place. The Reverend Henry Bull on a site that was once a monastery built the Rectory.

That explains the spectral nun that the whole Bull family saw on numerous occasions; indeed, the Reverend Bull used to sit many hours in the summer house on the lawn - in fact he erected it - to watch the spectral nun swaying gently along the wall.

Let me now explain why there is a ghostly nun. The monastery, over which the Rectory was built, housed a religious order of both monks and nuns. In this case it also housed Cupid for a monk eloped with one of the nuns. They were soon caught and brought back to be punished for being so sinful. How can that be sinful when a man and woman fall in love? That surely, is what God intended. If you do not look at an attractive

Signorina – I am in Italy – then you are not normal. I have five doing the work of one … Bella. I digress.

They were normal and for that the monk was hanged. They spared him the pain of being drawn and quartered. The poor nun also paid with her life but she was given time to repent, not that it did her much good, for she was bricked up alive inside one of the walls.

The spectral nun returned – rightly so, you must agree – to haunt the monastery, as she searched in vain for her lover. Even with the monastery gone, the ghostly nun can still be seen gliding along an unseen path. When the Rectory was built the ghostly nun continued to appear and, even with the Rectory now gone … the spectral nun can still be seen.

When the Reverend Bull died in 1892, the Rectory was taken over by his son, the Reverend Harry Bull who had also seen the ghostly nun many times, the main time being on 28th July, the day when the cries from the wall were last heard.

After the demise of the Reverend Harry Bull in 1927, the Rectory remained vacant for no clergyman would live in the haunted place. In 1928, after being empty for over 12 months, the Reverend Eric Smith and his wife moved in. They were both non-believers in the paranormal but the spectral nun soon changed all that and the Reverend Smith even claimed that minutes after seeing the spectral nun disappear, he heard a woman's voice exclaim: 'Don't Carlos, don't!' That was enough for the Reverend Smith and his wife, they could not stay another minute and, they quickly left. They were very adamant that Borley Rectory was haunted, of that they were in no doubt. They had remained in the Rectory for just a year. It was they who first called in Harry Price to investigate the ghostly happenings.

After the Smith's came the Reverend Lionel Foyster and his wife in 1930 and, they remained at the Rectory for the next 5 years; throughout that period the ghostly happenings continued and on many occasions were witnessed by very reliable people.

Were they all liars? On one occasion Marianne Foyster was struck across the face by an unseen force. It was frightening and it drove the Foysters out.

In 1937 Harry Price leased the site for a year so that he could continue his investigations into the paranormal happenings. From his research Price produced a book about the Rectory.

At the end of 1938, Captain W.H. Gregson purchased Borley Rectory and in February 1939, some books fell over and knocked an oil lamp over, setting fire to the building. It was completely gutted.

Borley Rectory has gone but not so the spectral nun.

THE GHOST OF BLUE BELL HILL

In September 1933, Rochester Council purchased 105 acres of land between the Rochester-Maidstone and Chatham roads for the purpose of developing a municipal airport. Short Brothers, who had been in the area since 1913, then leased the land.

By the end of 1934 other firms had moved into Rochester and, air services were established on 9 June 1934 when Short's began a service from Rochester to Southend.

It is interesting to note - in today's 21st Century world of women in this and women in that at fever pitch - that in 1934 a small hangar was built for a private aircraft owner-pilot; by the name of Miss G. Batcheler; who, was the first woman in the country to have a pilot's license; and that was done without burning her bra.

Another young lady who did not have to burn her bra – she worn it as ear muffs – no only joking; was Miss Isabella Straton, who in January 1876, made the first winter ascent of Mont Blanc, the loftiest mountain (15,782 feet) in the entire chain of the Alps. That was some feat, when you consider that great glaciers stream from all sides of Mont Blanc.

In 1938 the Royal Air Force formed No. 23 Elementary and Reserve Flying School at Rochester. A second hangar was built in July 1938 when the school was expanded to train pilots for the Fleet Air Arm; during 1939 the factory was extended and the mighty four-engined Stirling bomber started to be produced at

Rochester. This made Rochester a main Luftwaffe target and, on 15 August 1940, the airfield was attacked by enemy aircraft, resulting in severe damage to Short's factory and the destruction of six Stirling bombers on the production line.

On the night of the air raid, a young lady set out from Maidstone on the main road, to cycle back to Rochester, to see her boyfriend who worked at Rochester airfield; situated south-east of Rochester between the B2097 and the A229 roads. Just before she reached Blue Bell Hill, her chain broke. In sheer desperation to get to Rochester airfield she ran out to stop a lorry; but on the wartime dipped lights, the driver did not see her and she received a glancing blow - knocking her to the ground and, it was alleged she fell under the back wheels of the lorry.

A few months after the accident a person reported running over a young lady at Blue Bell Hill but when he got out to offer help ... she had vanished.

Over the years dozens of people have reported running over a young lady... only to find it is the Ghost of Blue Bell Hill. I have also received many letters; saying that the ghost of a young lady is seen in the middle of the road ... only to vanish before those who have seen here are able to stop.

THE LINDBERGH GHOSTS

He was born at Detroit on 4 February 1903, of Swedish descent; and he entered the Air Mail Service of the U.S.A. flying from St. Louis to Chicago, after being at the army flying schools in Texas for two years. In May 1927, he became known by his non-stop solo flight across the Atlantic. It was, and still is, one of the greatest flights of all time. This was achieved in a Ryan Brougham single-engine, high wing monoplane, which the pilot Charles

Charles Augustus Lindbergh in front of his famous aircraft, the Spirit of St. Louis.

Augustus Lindbergh had specially modified. A keen and skilful pilot, Lindbergh fancied his chances at the $25,000 prize for the first non-stop flight between New York, America and Paris, France. With the financial backing of a group of St. Louis businessmen (hence his aircraft being called 'Spirit of St. Louis'), Lindbergh got his chance, and showed the world, he could do it. He flew non-stop from New York to Paris in 33 hours 50 minutes; the first airman to fly the Atlantic alone; but was he alone?

What is not often spoken about, and was not shown in the film with James Stewart, of this famous flight, was Lindbergh's belief in ghosts. On that famous flight Lindbergh recalls a moment when his cockpit was filled with ghosts. He said they were transparent, floating and weightless, friendly shadows that talked to him, and talked shop, especially navigational problems. They would mass up behind him, then there would only be two, their voices coming from very far, but trying to calm him and saying things, giving information which could not be obtained in real life.

Lindbergh firmly believed in these, and fact, he was able to achieve what others had failed. Were these friendly ghosts always with him when he flew? And had Lindbergh believed in ghosts even before his flight, hence the word 'Spirit' in the name of his aircraft 'Spirit of St. Louis' having more than one meaning?

In 1929 Colonel Lindbergh married a daughter of Dwight Morrow, late ambassador to Mexico. In 1932, Lindbergh's baby son was kidnapped and murdered. Sadly Lindbergh's friendly ghosts could not help him for their powers were in flight, for in the air it was as though Lindbergh was protected, and though he was a consultant to industrial firms in the early part of World War Two, he was later to fly fifty combat missions. It seems that it was here that the ghosts could help him. Maybe because their Spirits were in the sky… the sky they loved, as did Colonel Charles Lindbergh.

But whatever, they were there for him whenever he flew. Lindbergh was not alone in his beliefs; a classic case being Flying Officer Bill Corfield – see 'Saved by the Ghost of His Brother' in **Ghost Stations™4**.

Even Baron von Richthofen (The Red Baron) spoke about a ghost he encountered while mountain climbing with his younger brother, though I do not know if this ghost had anything to do with flying. Who can say with the human soul? There is no doubting the great passion and love that a pilot feels for the air, as a sailor does for the sea, any one who has read High Flight – see **Ghost Stations™** Poems - can see this passion. Is it this, which in the Spirit World holds them to their great love and their will to help fellow pilots or sailors?

Who can tell?

AN ENCOUNTER OF THE THIRD KIND

In July 1959, Brandon White, and his school chum, Alan Hinson, decided they would have a touring holiday on a tandem. They were both keen on aircraft and planned a plane-spotting tour to take in Chelveston, Alconbury, Wyton, Bedford (Thurleigh), Wittering and Upwood.

They set off from Lutterworth, riding a tandem loaded down with camping equipment and arrived at Chelveston airfield in Northamptonshire for their first stop. The two young lads looked over the airfield for a suitable camp site to set up their tent for the night. They soon found a suitable meadow at the north end of the airfield.

Chelveston airfield opened as a bomber station in August 1941, but the following year, the Americans took over the airfield and it became home for B-17 bombers. The American bombers took part in many daylight raids, suffering their biggest losses in a raid against Schweinfurt, in Germany, on 14th October 1943. The 305th Bomb Group from Chelveston lost 13 aircraft on that raid and it had been a heavy price to pay. Some badly shot up B-17's made it back only to crash attempting to land.

After the war, the airfield was handed back to the Royal Air Force. Then, in the early 1950's, the United States Air Force took over and laid a new runway for the 3914th Air Base Group for American B-47 bombers. For Brandon White and his chum, Alan

Hinson, Chelveston was an excellent choice as to where to start their plane-spotting holiday … but, it was to be one that they would never forget, as Brandon explains:

"At the North end of the airfield, six silver RB66 aircraft sat parked along dispersals glittering in the evening sunshine. We pitched our tent in a field close to the aeroplanes, hoping that come morning, we'd see them in action. After our trusty primus stove had given us both food and drink, we were preparing to turn in for the night when an old man approached us asking what we were up to. We told him of our plans to tour the airfields we had in mind and that we were both members of the Royal Observer Corps and how aircraft recognition was important to ROC members, he eventually left us after repeating several times 'I wouldn't camp here, if I were you.'

"Some time later, as the twilight was giving way to darkness, we heard the unmistakable sound of an American petrol engined heavy truck arriving in the farm track bordering our chosen field. The lane was a dead end and the truck turned round and stopped at the gateway to our field about fifty yards away. An American, dressed in 'fatigues' climbed out of the truck wearing the round type baseball cap and was looking at us and our tent. We expected to be ordered off the field, but instead of reprimanding us, the serviceman lit a large fire and began bellowing, HO! HO! HO! in a way designed to cause alarm. The fire, we surmised, must have been caused by petrol as the hedgerow began crackling, at this time the driver of the truck could

81

clearly be seen waving his arms and still shouting HO! HO! in a manner country folk use to shepherd or herd cattle. Then, as suddenly as it began, the fire died out, the driver climbed back into the truck, - which was the canvass back type - and drove away ... so our tent stayed in place."

Brandon and his pal, Alan, were very bewildered ... all was quiet. They were too tired to up tent and find a new site so they decided to stay, but sleep with one eye open. They eventually turned in for the night and the rest of the night passed un-eventfully.

The next morning, they were both up early and, after a quick look over the RB66's, they packed up their gear and headed to the other side of the airfield. They left the meadow by the same gate that they had entered, discussing the warning that they had received the night before, and they both looked along the hedgerow of the lane for traces of the fire that they had both so clearly seen ... but there was no sign of having been any fire ... their hearts beat faster. "The grass and the hedge where the fire had been was as green and normal as it should be," said Brandon, "there was no sign of burning."

Brandon and Alan continued on their plane-spotting tour and, thankfully, the rest of their holiday was without encounters of the third kind. What had they witnessed that summer evening in 1959?

As the years passed, it slipped from the mind of Brandon White ... until one evening in 1984. He had attended a film show at Grafton Underwood Village

Hall and, during the evening, he overheard a conversation that brought it all flooding back, as Brandon recalls:

"I overheard conversation from the seats behind about the strange goings on at Chelveston airfield concerning an American Ambulance that roams the airfield at night and the antics of people trying to see the vehicle."

He sat unable to believe his ears ... and he relived again ... that summer night in 1959, when he and his friend Alan Hinson, witnessed an encounter of the third kind.

THE HAUNTINGS AT RAF DEBDEN

When I interviewed Ex-Corporal Upton, regarding the RAF Scampton incidents, I naturally asked him if he had experienced any other unexplainable events on any other RAF Stations. "I can recall others but they are all hearsay." he said. He then went on to say:

"But there is another I can give you first-hand. When I was at RAF Debden in 73-74, it was during the oil crisis. I was made the Energy Orderly for the Barrack Blocks. Two out of every three light bulbs had been removed and my job was to go round last thing every night and switch off the remainder. So I was always last in bed.

"One night I had just got into bed and I was looking across the room in the direction of a friend who was asleep. When all of a sudden … he jumped up screaming. When he had calmed down he said he had seen an airman leaning over him.

"The whole Barrack Block, was by this time awake and several others, also said that they had seen an airman on several occasions, wandering around the billet late at night. Although I was looking directly at Bob when he jumped up … I saw no one there.

"The next day I went to the Guardroom to find why someone; was patrolling our billet in the middle of the night. I was told that at no time had anyone been there. They just did not do that."

RAF Debden in Essex had been an important airfield during the Second World War and. had played a major role in the Battle of Britain. It was attacked many times by the Luftwaffe. The airfield was transferred to the United States Army Air Force in September 1942. In the run-down period after the war, Debden had a training role and, in 1960 became the RAF Police Depot, until closure of the station in April 1975.

During his period at Debden, Steve Upton tried to solve some of the mysteries. The old wartime airfield certainly had an 'air-of-uneasy-feeling' about it … .a feeling that one should not be there, as Upton explains:

"Debden still showed signs of war damage, bullet holes in many walls were commonplace. I was told that the WRAF Block had been hit and quite a few WRAF's killed. The Block had not been rebuilt; because whenever builders started work on it, tools just disappeared and various other things happened to make them abandon the job. That was why one of the H-Blocks was incomplete."

So Debden joins the long list of haunted airfields … did the wartime propaganda machine smooth over the cracks? It is a fact that Debden Airfield came under heavy attack in August 1940; and a great deal of damage was done. Many buildings were destroyed; and in one attack, five people were listed as killed … but were there more? Yes, there were certainly more.

THE OLD PARSONAGE HOTEL

"Just walked into the bar at the Old Parsonage and there it was … a figure of a woman," said Jeff Smithson. "She was sort of greyish white … like a hazy look … sort of floated towards me then turned and disappeared before my eyes. It was a ghost alright."

The Old Parsonage Hotel and Restaurant at Crewkerne in Somerset, is reputed to be haunted. Had Jeff Smithson seen a ghost?

The Old Parsonage has had many sightings of a ghostly figure of a woman, which has become known as the White Lady, and it certainly has the history to attract a ghost.

As the name suggests, the building was originally the Parsonage to Crewkerne's famous 15th century church. Indeed, a secret tunnel to the church is rumoured to exist, but then, the tunnel from the church to the mansion stories, related to about almost every village in England. But in this story, there is much more than a germ of truth in the secret passage.

The building is partly 15th and partly 18th Century, and is of great historical and architectural interest. It is also of great interest regarding the mysterious White Lady ghost … and the secret passage.

Bill and Betty Bennet called in the summer of 1982. "Bill had just gone to wash his hands … suddenly I felt cold and I glanced into the comer of the room," said Betty. "I could not believe my eyes … a whitish hazy light sort of appeared through the wall and as it moved into the room, I could see it was a woman. It was clearly a shape of a woman and whilst I stared at her she vanished right before my eyes."

Side View of the Old Parsonage Hotel. It was through this side wall on the ground floor that the ghostly White Lady was seen to come through.

Betty felt rooted to the spot and she had not even heard her husband return. He sat and listened to what she had to say, then suggested a gin and tonic as a chaser to the other spirit. "It's not funny, it was there," said Betty. And she added: "Bill took it all too lightly and told me to forget it."

In 1984, Mrs. Winifred Grant got in touch with me after reading Ghosts that haunt our old airfields, in the Sunday Mercury. She wrote to say that she was interested in finding out more about the ghost that is said to haunt the Old Parsonage Hotel, after she and her husband had stayed a weekend there in August 1984. The Old Parsonage was then run by John and Therise Bolt, who had been there under twelve months.

So is the Old Parsonage haunted? It has certainly changed hands many times. Does the White Lady hold the answer to the reason why?

On the Sunday evening, Winifred's husband went for a walk around the village. He got into conversation with two of the locals, who informed him that the Old Parsonage was haunted and asked ... if he had seen the ghost.

Mr. Grant told his wife and the next morning she asked the landlord about the ghost. "He said there had been two sightings of it during the last twelve months; but he did not say he had seen it," said Mrs. Grant.

"He said one sighting was, he believed, genuine. It was seen in the Hotel Bar - a white shape, possibly a lady - by a man, a complete stranger who had only been in the hotel five minutes and had never been in the area before."

As previously stated, the Old Parsonage was once the dwelling place of a parson. He was in charge of the tithe barn, which is across the road, and has, today, been converted into two houses and two flats, which gives some indication of its original size. During the war, Americans were billeted in the house. So there is some wartime connection. It is said that the original stone roof was sold to America. That could be true, for after the war the tithe barn had a galvanized tin roof.

The two little cottages that nestle at the side of the Old Parsonage were build around 1801, and presumably once belonged to the Parsonage when it was a farm. The cottages were sold back to the Parsonage when it was converted to a hotel some time after 1959.

Mr. Davies was born in one of the little cottages near the Old Parsonage: "My mother and myself were born in those cottages and we grew up there," he said. "My grandmother, who owned the two cottages, was born in 1887, just around the corner in Tower Hill Road." And, he added: "I have never heard my grandmother, mother, or anyone, ever mention a ghost in the parsonage, and believe for one reason or another that it's a modem invention."

Side View of the Old Parsonage Hotel

The Old Parsonage Hotel at Crewkerne - seen here without the ghostly White Lady- February 1988. This grandeur front is 18th Century. Note: Nestling against the Old Parsonage is Mr. Davies Grandmother's cottage. If you look at the roof on the little cottage you will see that the bottom part has its original Somerset stone tiled roof.

But that does not mean to say that the Old Parsonage is not haunted. Different people have reported seeing a ghost of a Lady and that could be the reason for change of ownership ... but what about the secret passage? That could be true; but Mr. Davies has his doubts about that too, as he explains: "There has always been talk about a mysterious passage that was supposed to run from the cellars, to the church … and I have always been interested in the stories.

"The cottages were only two-up two-down affairs, but in our living room floor there was either a crack in the floor or a loose stone. This gave rise that there could be a secret passage. But I never ever saw the floor because, after the fashion of those days, it was covered with linoleum. Anyway, if one trod on this crack or loose stone … it moved.

"I often said: 'Oh granny, is that the secret passage?' and visitors would often remark so. My grand- mother was always adamant that no passage, secret or otherwise, ran from the house and she always maintained that, as a child, she had seen the entrance to a passage in one of the barns opposite. This was supposed to have been uncovered by workmen, and when they had finished, it was covered in again."

So, we now ask: … Is there a ghost? … And is there a secret passage? … And if so, are they linked to the church? It is a mystery and one who would like it solved is Louise M. Brazier, who wrote to me in November 1987: "We are the proprietors of the Old Parsonage, having acquired it some six months ago. We have, of course, heard many stories of the sightings of the White Lady, as she is known, but no one seems to know the origin of her existence."

We have heard that Mr. Davies thought a secret passage most unlikely but, on the other hand, he did say he never saw the floor and, there was a crack or loose stone. That could have been the secret passage; if not, what was it? Not a cellar in only a two-up two-down cottage ... that is for sure. And you do not get smoke without fire ... and Mr. Davies said: "My grandmother was always adamant that no passage, secret or otherwise, ran from the house."

But that would be a natural reaction, for it could be very dangerous to have children looking for the secret passage. So, with children around, it would be only wise, to deny any secret passage ever existed, in order to stop them looking for it.

Would it have been possible for a secret passage? Yes, but difficult. Barn Street descends quite steeply and, at the time the secret passage would have been built, the land at the bottom could well have been marshy. Therefore, a tunnel would have had to be dug to a great depth. Not impossible though. But it would have needed much more labour and would then hardly have been secret. Still, that is not impossible; for secret tunnels do exist – I know of a great many – and I think it quite possible that there is a secret passage. Its location and age make it a good bet that there is one. One does have to know how and where to look; and I speak from experience. But Mr. Davies said: "If such an entrance ever existed, then I think my grandmother, probably saw the entrance to some sort of cellar."

That, I doubt. It was not a cellar. I am certain that the secret passage is there ... as for the White Lady, I will leave to the regulars of The Old Parsonage after a few gin and tonics and a good day on the horses, it might be possible to see the White Lady.

THE GHOSTS OF THE SOUTH CHINA SEAS

After the Second World War Captain (later Major) Robert Keith Jones was with a War Graves Unit serving with War Crimes Investigation. "I had, or met, several odd occurrences with first hand knowledge which, I can only describe as supernatural," he said. "There can be no doubt that some force occasionally manifests itself which, the layman either rejects, or, accepts as the supernatural."

Major Jones has been all over the Far East, following Service in Burma and, is one of the very few who have been all over Java, Sumatra, Malaya, Burma, the Death Railway, and most of the lands and islands in the South China Seas looking for evidence of war crimes.

He explains for my readers: "I should explain the job entailed a vast amount of investigation as to how soldiers and civilians had met their death during the Japanese occupation of the Far East. As many as possible were exhumed from their far flung graves and re-interred in the massive cemetery at Singapore and, if some were found to be buried with their hands tied behind their backs they had obviously not died from natural causes.

"During this particular incident in 1946 I was based at Singapore; I was provided with a 61 foot RASC motor launch, capable of about 8 knots maximum speed, with an army crew of four men - the skipper being a corporal. My instructions were to investigate some burials on various Islands south of Singapore and, as far south as the Sunda Straits - between Java and Sumatra. In fact, on this particular occasion, I landed on every one of the Islands in the Rhio and Linga Archipelago. The sea was like a millpond for the whole month of my stay afloat, the sun was high and bright every day and, nothing happened which was in any way out of the ordinary. Besides the crew of four, my party consisted of myself in charge of the operation, a Staff Sergeant and four British other ranks, all of whom were trained soldiers who had been through the war in Burma, were intelligent men and, amenable to discipline.

Captain Robert Keith Jones in Western Sumatra.

Chinese prisoners being buried alive by the Japanese.

This picture shows Japanese army recruits being instructed in the use of the bayonet with prisoners as targets.

More human targets for Japanese soldiers. This photograph was smuggled out of Shanghai. Plenty of proof for Captain Jones ... but they were never made to pay for their war crimes.

A specific task was to find and recover the remains of an Australian Nurse and Doctor suspected of being murdered by the Japanese in 1941. I had been given the names of the victims and the Island on which they were buried and, they were quickly dubbed Frankie and Johnny by the crew. The bodies were recovered, or what few bones remained of them, each was wrapped in a blanket, tied with wire, labelled and, placed one on each bow seat of the launch, protected by the bow but, otherwise open to the sky. They had been buried side by side on the Island with Frankie on the left and Johnny on the right, according to which end of the graves they were viewed but, such was their state of decomposition it was impossible to tell which was which. They were placed in the same relative positions on the bow seats, in distinctive blankets, so that even had the labels been washed off, or the remains dislodged during heavy seas - which one normally expects in the South China Seas - we would know which was which. Further, the crew and, my own men, were given strict orders that the bow position of the launch was out of bounds except in an emergency and on the orders of the Skipper. And, to make it very clear, I then drew a white line across the deck, six feet back from the bows, so that all on board knew the area that was 'out of bounds', We then started back to Singapore.

Drawing of the boat by Captain Jones to show position of corpse on the bow seats. Note. The steel wire used to tie the corpse was field cable.

"The following morning the position of the blankets containing the remains were reversed, i.e., Frankie was on the right and Johnny on the left. I returned them to the original position, called the men together and told them that I was displeased that my order had not been obeyed. All assured me that no-one had been near the bows and, the Skipper added two points - 1) that sailors were superstitious and would not go near dead bodies anyway - in fact my own men had to do all the handling - and, 2) that he had been on the bridge all night, that it had been bright moonlight all the time, that the bow of the launch had been in full view of the wheelhouse all the time and, that no-one on board had been further forward than the bridge (amidships).

"Nothing happened all that day but, the following morning the position of the remains had again been reversed. Once again, I returned the remains to their original position, called the men together and, expressed in strong terms that I considered someone was playing a joke, that I did not see the funny side and, left them in no doubt as to what would happen if they did it again. I was nevertheless assured that nobody had been near the bows. Their protestations were so strong, not to say indignant, that I discussed the matter at some length with my Staff Sergeant and, we decided to remain on watch together all that night. We both accepted the fact that the crew were not to blame and, that our own men would not play such a practical joke in contravention of a direct military order. I may add that the relationships between everyone on board, including myself, were most cordial and, there was no alcohol consumed while sailing. What little canned beer we had was locked up at sea. We were on the return trip to Singapore, with several days sailing ahead of us.

"Nothing happened all day but, the following morning the position of the remains were again found to be reversed. Neither my Staff Sergeant or myself had seen or heard anything; nobody had come on deck; we had remained all night watching the remains, talking and smoking; we were observed by the Skipper from the wheelhouse all the time and, there was no possibility of all three of us having even dozed, let alone fallen asleep.

"Perhaps there is a supernatural force at work."

Strange ... But true. But that is not the end of the story. Let me first add that Captain Jones and his men were at sea for a total of one month - two weeks out and two weeks back to Singapore. That would mean, after other calls, about one week with the corpses which, were handed over to the War Graves Authorities in Singapore.

Major Jones returned to England in 1948 and, many times pondered over the strange eerie incident of Frankie and Johnny. In 1966 he sent to General T.C. Lethbridge at the institute of Psychic Research.

"I received a long reply dated 27 July 1966," said Major Jones, "in which he said that the whole thing was perfectly natural - normal - and probably a seaman with 'small powers' had wished the corpses elsewhere but only managed to change their positions."

That I do not accept, nor did Major Jones. To do it once ... might be able to think it was the answer. But to do it six times ... you must look for a supernatural answer.

Lethbridge based his reply on Professor Rhine's research. He said that he had reasonably demonstrated that such things can be done by mental power alone. Thus the incident of Frankie and Johnny can be classified under the heading of poltergeist phenomena. And, said he would plump for one of the superstitious crew who, was unknowingly responsible for changing the positions of the corpses.

But that answer I do not accept, for it is the Supernatural World that provides the answer to the Ghosts of the South China Seas.

TRYING TO EXPLAIN THE UNEXPLAINED

The Ghosts of the South China Seas – that you have just read about in the previous story – was such an eerie incident, that Major Jones could not stop thinking about it; and, he tried to find an explanation.

In 1966 he wrote to General T .C. Lethbridge and I briefly cover his reply in the previous story; you now have chance to read the letter which, I publish on the following pages; but first, let me explain about T .C. Lethbridge.

T .C. Lethbridge, known to his friends as Tom, was trained as an archaeologist and historian. He was for many years the Keeper of Anglo-Saxon Antiquities at the University Museum in Cambridge and, President of the Cambridgeshire Archaeological Society.

Lethbridge embarked on many strange studies and he was convinced that there are at least three kinds of magnetic field, with strange forces connected with each field; like another dimension. Lethbridge carried out dowsing with a pendulum, ridiculed at the time but now gives much food for thought. Lethbridge was at the door of discovery and found a scientific answer for events termed supernatural.

Lethbridge passed away in a Devon nursing home in 1971 ... having spent his whole life spent trying to explain the unexplained.

27th July 1966

BRANSCOMBE 229

HOLE HOUSE
BRANSCOMBE
Nr. SEATON
DEVON

Dear Captain Jones,

Many thanks for your letter which I
find most interesting. Although I get
a very large number of letters on this
subject, very few deal with the actual
moving of objects by unexplained means.
It has however been reasonably demonstrated
by Professor Rhine that such things can
be done by mental power alone. If this
is accepted, and it seemed to be conclusively
proved by a long series of most boring
experiments, then you have to look at things
in a different way. Your incident of
Frankie & Johnny can be classified under

the heading of poltergeist phenomena. I don't
go in for 'investing that sort of thing yet;
but I was asked to help to remove one
last year s, to my surprise, succeeded.
I don't think Frankie s Johnny themselves
had anything to do with it. The force
which moved the packages came from the
mental disturbance of one of the crew, or
of your burial party. I should plump
for one of the superstitious crew. The
people who cause poltergeists are usually
teenagers, mostly girls, or people who are
not very tightly screwed on. When subjected
to some mental strain the effects are
frequently violent s inexplicable. If you
had a member of the crew who was a
little bit 'sawn off' or underdeveloped, it

HOLE HOUSE
BRANSCOMBE
NR. SEATON
DEVON

BRANSCOMBE 229

is a safe bet that he was unknowingly responsible for changing the positions of the corpses.

I have been working at this subject now for a number of years & know a bit more about it than I did when I wrote Ghost & Ghoul — not much, but a bit. I do not believe in any of it being supernatural. It is all natural, but uninvestigated & one can treat it as a Scientific study. If it interests you I have two more books out: Ghost & Divining Rod & ESP which should be in a library & tell the story of how we have been working at the Subject. A third is nearly finished. My object is to try to find out what the force is which is used in all these phenomena. It is not electricity or magnetism but seems to be related to the Earth's mass. It can be built up by a number of worried people into something very strong. This, I think, is what happens with the Burmese 'nats's' such like supposedly evil spirits.

It is an extremely fascinating study but one must treat it with complete indifference to get results & be ready to throw over any theory in the face of new evidence. Most people start with ready formed beliefs & that is fatal to success.

Yours sincerely

T. C. Lethbridge

I have published the letter from T .C. Lethbridge for it is interesting to see it first-hand. From the original hand-written letter one can get a better picture of Lethbridge; and, I am certain that his many followers will find the contents of great interest. As stated, he spent his life trying to explain the unexplained.

THE RUDOLF HESS MYSTERY

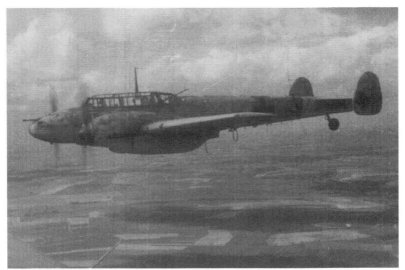

A Messerschmitt Bf 110

The Following is an official story told at the time:

It was a fine evening with a dull sky to the north. At 10.33 p.m. the traces of two unidentified aircraft were picked up by a gun operations room in east Scotland. They were plotted as approaching the coast from the south of the Faroe Islands. As they neared land they separated, one turning north and the other continuing overland in a westerly direction. This aircraft, which turned north, was soon identified as a friendly one; whereas the other was taken to be hostile.

The aircraft identified as hostile was again plotted flying due west to the south of Moffat at a height of

5,000 feet and again south of Cambuslang. Then the plotting near Busby and all trace was lost.

All gun and searchlight sites were standing by for the aircraft was getting dangerously near Glasgow. At 11.00p.m. the spotter on a searchlight site about eight miles south of the city saw an aircraft clearly in the moonlight. He immediately identified it as an Me.110. The warning was flashed to the heavy guns at Glasgow.

At 11.07 p.m. a neighbouring site again caught a glimpse of the aircraft still flying west. As they watched, it turned and began to circle the site. The pilot seemed to be checking his position. Twice it circled round the site. The air was quiet, the pilot had switched off his engine; and then, to everybody's consternation, he took a shallow dive straight at the site. From the aircraft a parachute streamed out. Some thought, with subsequently growing conviction, that they had seen a man silhouetted against the moonlight as he baled out. Others thought they were being dived-bombed. All thought their last moment had come, but just when the aircraft was about to strike the site it turned off, crashed to the ground not 250 yards away and burst into flames. This was the telephonist's great moment. He proudly reported the affair to headquarters while the detachment formed two parties, one to attend to the burning aircraft, the other to hunt the parachutist.

Meanwhile, the two A.A. signalmen, hearing the crashing aircraft, had come running out of their quarters in time to see the pilot floating slowly to earth. Half-dressed, they rushed towards the place where they knew there was a small farmhouse. When they reached it, the back door opened and a ploughman appeared.

"Are you looking for a parachutist?" he inquired.

They said they were.

"Well, he's inside now, arrived about half a minute ago," said the ploughman.

They dashed into the cottage. There in an armchair, dressed in a fleece-lined brown leather-flying suit, sat the parachutist. He threw out his hands to prove they were empty, and said, "Ah! British soldiers – no guns – no bombs." They immediately searched him for weapons, but found none. The prisoner said that his aircraft was unarmed. They asked his name. "Alfred Horn," he replied: and as they could not understand him properly he wrote it down on a piece of paper.

"Where have you come from?" they asked him. He replied, "Munich in four hours."

One of the soldiers went to telephone headquarters for a car to remove Alfred Horn, whose ankle was apparently injured by his fall. The other soldier looked curiously at the prisoner, for he had heard much about the poor quality of German clothes. There was nothing of this in the clothing Alfred Horn wore. His fleece-lined suit and boots were of good leather. He wore a gold wristwatch, and carried what looked like a Leica camera round his neck. A map with his course roughly plotted was strapped round his knee.

He asked if he might keep his parachute as a souvenir. The soldier gave a non-committal reply and asked him if he had ever been to England before. "No," he replied; and after a pause, "I have a very important message for the Duke of Hamilton." Whom he said he had met at the Berlin Olympic Games. He seemed to want to be friendly, and showed them a picture of his wife and son with whom he said he had spent the morning. One of the soldiers asked him if he would like to return to Germany if he got the chance. He immediately shouted, "No! No! No!"

The scene where the aircraft had crashed was increasingly confused. There were policemen, the Fire Brigade, the A.F.S; the Home Guard, soldiers from neighbouring units, RAF men and many civilians. The searchlight detachment were ordered to fix bayonets, and even then had great difficulty in clearing the field. Many pieces of the aircraft had disappeared into cars in which spectators had arrived, but these were eventually all recovered and handed over. Its machine guns were brand new. There was no ammunition, and the gun barrels were filled with grease.

One of the gunners, on return from escorting the prisoner, had a strong idea that he had seen a photograph of him recently. Every newspaper and magazine to hand were diligently scanned, and suddenly the gunner shouted, "That's him! I'm sure that's him." He pointed to a photograph of a dark, strongly built man, a Nazi, with thick black hair and deep-set eyes. It was a photograph of Rudolf Hess, Hitler's Deputy. How they all laughed.

Their troop officer had been sent to the Home Guard Headquarters, where an RAF Intelligence

Officer was interrogating the prisoner, assisted by a crowd of officers and others. The contents of the prisoner's pockets were emptied out on to the desk, including two hypodermic syringes, a phial of liquid and two bottles of white tablets. The troop officer turned to the RAF officer who was at the moment doing the interrogating, and said:

"You know, sir, I believe this is Rudolf Hess. I've seen him in Germany, and I recognise him as Hess."

"Don't be a fool," he was told.

He wasn't being. And so ends the early official story.

The more you think about Deputy Fuhrer Rudolf Hess - the mystery deepens. Returning by car from Italy to England, I went via Germany and stayed a few days with my good friend Ulrich. He took me for the usual night out and introduced me to a former Luftwaffe pilot. And, throughout the evening, I not only digested the Wiener schnitzel, but also what he told me about Rudolf Hess. And, it has made me look again at the facts that we have to hand.

The former Luftwaffe pilot said that the British Intelligence fabricated the whole story. Adolf Hitler had been informed of the plan right from the start. By now Hess had served his purpose and his aircraft was intercepted and shot down, possibly by Oberstleutnant Heinz Bar. An interesting conversation, and it does appear that the British were expecting someone special to drop in during the early months of 1941; and I do mention this in my books on Lincolnshire.

Looking at the photographs of the wreckage of the mysterious Rudolf Hess's Messerschmitt Bf 110 long-range fighter - this by the way was not an aircraft for fools, its fuel system was very complicated and wide open to misuse, as with most German aircraft - you will see that the cockpit section is missing. Why?

And why was RAF Intelligence in such a tearing hurry to remove the wreckage from Number 63 Maintenance Unit? The cockpit section is still supposed - repeat, supposed, to be kept under lock and key by the RAF somewhere! What was so special about the cockpit? Was it fitted with dual controls? Was it flown to Scotland by someone else who went to ground after bailing out? And what was the other aircraft that was tracked coming in with Hess and then peeled off and headed north, yet was identified as friendly?

Hess could have bailed out of a British aircraft, or, someone else could have bailed out and the mysterious Hess could have arrived on the scene. The whole operation could have been made to look like a home-guard exercise. It is said that a farm worker called David Mclean - armed only with a pitchfork – was the one who claimed to have arrested Hess; but not in the official first story you have just read.

The wreckage of the mysterious Hess does not look as if it has just crashed. It does not look fresh. Remember, it was supposed to be a new aircraft, yet this wreckage looks as if it has been lying around a scrap yard for months. The ground does not look to show any impact of a crash. The wreckage looks to have been put there to add credibility to the story. The bits could have come from other Messerschmitt Bf 110's. And the radio call sign on the fuselage VJ +OQ could have been painted on or, even altered. And to make everyone think that it was Deputy Führer Rudolf Hess, a story was leaked about three SS Parachutists who were supposed to have arrived to murder Hess. This was another fabrication.

The <u>claimed</u> wreckage Rudolf Hess's Messerschmitt Bf 110

To study the photographs of the wreckage you will notice that the fabric covering of the rudders and elevators is missing. It is stripped clean. Could army souvenir hunters have done this when there were lots of cotton bits and pieces to pick up? A small fire was reported. But not near the tail section. And I failed to notice a swastika on the fins of the mysterious Hess's aircraft.

Let us look at the flying kit of the mysterious Hess. Surely, that must be straightforward. But no, here the mystery only deepens. For a start, a Mae-West life jacket is conspicuous by its absence. A Mae-West is a must for over water flying. And the flight-path for the mysterious Hess was over an awful lot of water.

A picture taken on 9 October 1945 when the mysterious Hess was being interrogated by Colonel John Amen at Nuremberg, shows Hess in some of his flying kit. Yet an official statement said that the flying kit and all Hess's personal belongings had been destroyed. As former president Bush senior would say – "Read my Lips."

In December 1988 it was made known that Rudolf Hess's flying kit and other items were coming up for auction. But lo and behold ... the sale had to be cancelled. Why? Fear that something could have been hidden in them? It was said that they were stolen and a British officer at Spandau prison was charged with theft and extortion; therefore, a Court Martial. Never heard about it. What happened to the flying kit?

The files just recently released on Rudolf Hess told you nothing. The files now on view to the public are letters supposed to have been written by Ruldolf Hess about his food being poisoned.

The more you read ... the more it smells like a cover up. It is said Hess kept trying to commit suicide. If that was so, why bother to write saying the food is poisoned. And the final touch - Goodbye letters to Hitler, his wife and children. Very touching but not at all convincing.

113

On 10 May 1991, fifty years since Hess's flight to Scotland, I once more took a look at the Hess Mystery, which was only fitting to mark the 50th Anniversary of Hess's flight to Scotland.

Rudolf Hess died in the British Military Hospital in West Berlin shortly after being found unconscious with an electrical cord around his neck, in a summerhouse in the garden of Spandau Prison. Rotten to the end, no, not Hess, but the Allies and in particular the British Establishment that allowed this fiasco and travesty of justice and fair play. I say British Establishment, for the British people themselves felt this was wrong.

Hess, who had trained with the Imperial Flying Corps, took off in a Messerschmitt Bf 110 fighter, which was fitted with long-range tanks, that night in May 1941 and headed for Scotland. Very careful plans had been made for his peace mission. As Hitler's right-hand man, private secretary and deputy he was risking all in his attempt to negotiate peace terms, which is claimed to be with the Duke of Hamilton; and, let us remember, Hitler was winning the war at this stage. The German war machine had the sweet smell of victory in the air. Hess brought with him a list of top British people ... and there were many ... that he thought would be interested in his effort. He also brought with him Top Secret documents.

It was an excellent piece of navigation to locate the Lanarkshire estate of the Duke of Hamilton ... yet little or no credit was ever given to this fact. Hess baled out and he broke his ankle on landing, a farm worker found him hobbling around. Hess was taken to Eaglesham Police Station. He immediately requested to see the Duke of Hamilton who he claimed he had met during the 1936 Olympic games in Berlin, but this meeting of 1936 was later denied.

After many telephone calls, Hess, who had assumed a pseudonym, said he was Hauptmann Alfred Horn, until he was eventually interviewed by the Duke of Hamilton; who by the way, could not speak German. Hess was placed in a Military Hospital in Stirlingshire. Hess later told the Duke of Hamilton, in the presence of Sir Ivone Kirkpatrick his proposals for peace. The Duke of Hamilton, was at this time in the RAF, but never saw active service, unlike my good friend Lord Ancaster; in fact Hamilton was Air Training Corp and only in Scotland.

Hess said Hitler would accept British hegemony in the empire if Britain would accept German hegemony in Europe, and return of the former German colonies. The British fleet and the German army would rule the world. What a prize ... and a ministry of information stated: "This strange bird of good omen that has dropped in our midst ... fifty time more value as a propaganda carrier." But it never turned out to be ... why? I explain later. The British government made no attempt to capitalize on their star prisoner. Why? What reason did the British government have for holding back with the propaganda machine? They could have had a field day ... but no. Churchill even forbade anyone to photograph Hess. Why? All in good time.

The British Army contemptuously dismissed Hess's collection of homeopathic medicines and one report noted; "Judging from his conversation he appears to be a health crank." Would they have said that about Prince Charles? I think not.

Churchill seized upon this and set out to discredit Hess …why? For some reason that is what Churchill set out to do from day one; and Hess was put in the care of several trick-cyclists (psychiatrists). Churchill had been told that the British public looked upon anyone as mad … mad; if they had to see trick-cyclists. That gave Churchill an excellent way out with no questions asked. Hess would be deemed to be mad. However, as one would expect from trick-cyclists; true to form, all of them came to different conclusions … mad, unstable mind, crazy, hypochondriac, paranoid, neurotic … the list was endless; and the trick-cyclists should know, for they are the biggest screwballs of all.

Yet this man who they alleged was crazy flew to Scotland. The timing of the flight and the point of crossing the British coast would indicate a very considerable degree of planning. It was wartime and the British coast was defended. Despite all this, Hess arrived where he had planned to do so. No mention of this by the mad trick-cyclists. They have trouble to find their way out of a room. Hess had flown from Augsburg to Scotland; and would have landed – some claim that he did – had he not mistaken the Defiants for Hurricanes when he sighted them climbing to intercept. Hess was then on the last leg of his journey and was just starting to look for Dungavel where he intended to land. All worked out to perfection and not what one would expect from a mad man. His reaction to bale out after sighting what he thought were hurricanes was the action of a sane man destined to complete his task. But that, they did not take into account. And we shall never know for access to his file is barred until 2017. What about the 30-year rule? That is your freedom in Britain.

Hess was removed to the tower and thence to Mytchett Place in Hampshire where Lord Beaverbrook interviewed him. Why Beaverbrook? He was a big friend of Churchill's. But it backfired for someone at Mytchett Place - with strong communist views - sent a copy of the interview to Stalin. So much for Churchill and his security.

But this did nothing to help Rudolf Hess; who was first imprisoned in Buchanan Castle, then the Tower of London and finally in a villa at Abergavenny in South Wales. It was stated he was kept at Aldershot … but not true. On 10 October 1945, Hess was taken to the Nuremberg war trials; and he was judged guilty of "preparing and waging aggressive war," and he was shown no mercy by his captors.

Why was Hess persecuted? Since 1966 when Hess's two fellow-prisoners, Baldur von Schirach – leader of the Hitler youth and Gauleiter of Vienna; and Albert Speer, Hitler's one-time minister of munitions and war production, were released; Hess lived on alone in the 600-cell Spandau prison.

It took 600 people … soldiers, doctors, cooks, and office staff, supplied by the four wartime allied powers. British, American, French and Russian teams took turns in guarding Hess … the lone man of Spandau.

Why did Churchill want Hess discredited and made out to be mad? Why was no one allowed to photograph Hess? That is the first thing they should have done, it was a wonderful propaganda coup; but Churchill said otherwise. All questions the British public … and indeed the world … now want answered.

Rudolf Hess brought with him some top-secret documents that are held by the British government and, as stated, will remain secret until the year 2017 … by then they will all be gone. What was the reason for no photographs? No photographs for Hess had undergone medical torture?

On Monday 17 August 1987 … the loneliest and most mysterious man in the world passed away. Over the years there had been many pleads for his release … all to no avail. Even Lord Shawcross, the British chief prosecutor at the Nuremberg war crimes tribunal … cut no ice with his plea that Hess should be released

Was Hess mad? No. So what kind of man was he? Walter Richard Rudolf Hess was born in Alexandria in 1894. His father was Bavarian Lutheran who had an export business in Egypt. At the age of 14 he was sent to school at Godesberg. He then returned to help in the family business. When the First World War broke out he was in Hamburg and he joined the 1st Bavarian

Infantry Regiment. He saw a lot of fighting and was wounded at Verdun and again on the Russian Front.

After getting a commission Hess realized an old ambition by getting into the Air Force; but the war was over and his father's business had been ruined. In Munich he joined The Thule Society, which planned to assassinate the German Prime Minister. Hess was arrested and he shared Hitler's imprisonment at Landsberg from 1923 to 1924, helping Hitler with Mein Kampf. When Hitler assumed power Hess was formally proclaimed Deputy and Minister of state. He was always a faithful servant. On Hess's death, the allies in West Berlin issued a detailed statement, which said that Hess had hanged himself with an electrical extension lead. Before the statement was issued the world was led to believe that Hess – a 93-year-old man – had killed himself by putting the electric light lead around his neck whilst in the summer house and drawing it tight.

The first post-mortem examination was carried out at the British Military Hospital in West Berlin by professor Malcolm Cameron, a British pathologist and he said that Hess had died from choking. The Allies then issued a statement that said that all the evidence, including a farewell note left by Hess, pointed to suicide.

Not true. Hess did not commit suicide and on hearing the news, Hess's son expressed doubts that his father had killed himself. Many other people had their doubts about the Hess suicide, one being Colonel Eugene Bird, who was a commandant at Spandau from 1963 to 1972. The former US Army Colonel said: "Hess was too old and infirm to be able to end his life by his own hands ... I simply don't believe it." And he added: "Why should Hess wait for the chance finding of an electrical cord when he wore both braces and shoe laces?" So who had Hess's blood on their hands? It is a fact that he did not commit suicide therefore he was murdered. Who gave the order to kill Hess?

A second post mortem examination on the body of Rudolf Hess was then performed at the Forensic Science Institute of Munich University at the order of his family. Doctor Alfred Seidl, the Hess family lawyer, said the examination had found pressure marks on Hess's neck

On Thursday 20 August 1987 Hess's coffin was flown to Grafenwohr US Air Force Base in Bravia by an RAF Hercules aircraft for burial in the family plot in Wunsiedel cemetery, a small town near the Czechoslovak border. Doctor Seidl ordered Hess's coffin to be opened after the flight from West Berlin and he said they found no marks on Hess's neck. Hess's son said: "We have found no trace of strangulation marks on his neck. We have serious doubts about the official version of his death."

So let us now have a look at things. The Allies had condemned Hess to a living death. Doctor Alfred Seidl said that he suspected that Hess's death had to do with secret documents that he had with him when he flew to Britain. These documents are held by the British government and will remain secret until the year 2017 ... and, by that time they will have all gone missing and there will be none to view ... just like the Log Book of Conquer that went 'missing' with Maggie Thatcher.

It was always claimed that the Russians refused Hess's release, but when Mikhail Gorbachev came to power that was to change, Hess was soon to be a free man, but not if certain parties had anything to do with it. In Spandau he could be controlled, but free ... never. The British Establishment knew that once free, Hess could give details about his mission and what was in those Top Secret documents. Some say this would have damaged Churchill's reputation, but I say it is more the case that it would have damaged powerful people in the Establishment and that would have included Royalty.

Many theories have been put forward, one was that it was not Hess but an impostor; but Hess's son Wolf-Rudiger discredited this story and the story advanced by Hess's son is the most plausible under the circumstances. His theory, which is close to what I have found so far, is that the British Secret Service had lured the Deputy Fuehrer to Britain. If you recall, my friend Ulrich said the British Intelligence fabricated the whole story. Germany was at that stage winning the war. Therefore, Hess flew to Britain under the protection of a White Flag. Hess came to talk peace. What about the Geneva Convention? The Red Cross was not even allowed to see Hess. Never a visit. The Red Cross was silenced. Hess was not given a chance ... Churchill saw to that as I have just shown. In 1990 Thatcher was shouting that Second World War criminals should be hunted down and brought to trial. Good, but let us first start with those who stole Conquer's Log Book. Then turn to those who blooded Hess's White Flag. That is why Churchill said no photographs and had it made known that Hess was mad. Hess was not mad and as far as I know he did not walk around naked, as Churchill was known to do; and that is someone mad.

Hess came under a White Flag and for that reason refused to recognize the legality of the Nuremberg Court. Nuremberg is a name that should have haunted Churchill ... as you will find out when you read **Ghost Stations™** Germany.

Hess at the Nuremberg Trials – He is seated Front Row, second from left with a book on his knee.

THE DAM BUSTERS CURSE

After intensive training, which lasted six weeks, Operation Chastise was launched on 16 May 1943 and the first Lancaster took off before 2130 hours from RAF Scampton in Lincolnshire.

Nineteen specially modified Lancasters - coded AJ - took part in the raid on the Möhne, Eder and Sorpe Dams.

Wing Commander Guy Gibson - centre left, hand in pocket - just after being told to form a special squadron, number 617 Dam Busters.

The plan was for Wing Commander Guy Gibson's nine aircraft to attack all three dams, while a diversionary force of five Lancasters attacked the Sorpe and five Lancasters remained in reserve. Dropping their

Barnes Wallis spinning mines - nicknamed the bouncing bombs - at 220 miles-per-hour and, at exactly sixty feet, the squadron breached the Möhne and Eder Dams. Nigger, the code message announcing the success of the operation, was received at St Vincents, Grantham, and the Headquarters of No 5 Group, Bomber Command.

So much has been said and written about this flight to glory by No 617 Squadron's dams raid. We do know that eleven aircraft out of nineteen got back and fifty-three brave young men died. Guy Gibson lived to fight another day; but he was cursed for inflicting such terrible damage and slaughter of innocent men, women, children and, animals.

For the first time we now look at the dams raid from the German side and, photographs of the aftermath are shown in this volume for the first time.

From the following, one can get the picture at the Air Raid Warning Centre Vl/15 during the night of Monday 17 May 1943, as from 0030 hours.

The following is an actual translation of the official original Luftschutz - AR WC report.

0030 air raid alarm proposed, sounded at 0031 for Kassel
0034 air raid alarm for south group (Melsungen) 0035 break in the warning net due to battery short-out
0047 Kassel control reported 0045 4 - 6 enemy aircraft at position 82 - target not as yet discernible
0054 Dortmund control reported that at 0051 approx. 8 enemy aircraft circling in areas 823 and 825

0056 Kassel control reported enemy aircraft remaining in 82 on various courses

0100 Momentary report: aircraft activity at 72 and 82

0102 enemy aircraft circling in the Eder Dam area, still no object discernible

0106 Usseln aircraft spotters reported aircraft sounds at 10

0112 Air raid alarm sounded for eastern area report received that the Möehne Dam had been hit

0117 and 0118 reports received from aircraft spotters at Winterberg and at Waldeck concerning flares being dropped. The bearings of these reports suggested the Eder reservoir area(!)

0120 power restored to the warning circuit

0130 4 enemy aircraft reported dropping flares over the Eder reservoir

0138 smoke (steam) reported over the dam. Questions also to our unit at the Eder reservoir could, unfortunately, offer no explanation

0149 the dropping of flares continues

0155 further observance of aircraft circling over the Eder reservoir

0205 sounds of aircraft and searchlights over the dam and

0220 the ARP centres at Waldeck and Usseln report aircraft sounds.

When at the Kassel centre it was known that the Möhne reservoir (dam) had been hit. Special attention was paid to the activities of the enemy aircraft in the Eder (Kassel) area.

The continuous circling and the dropping of numerous flares indicated that the Eder Dam would be the target this night.

In answer to numerous telephone queries concerning the position from the police, the local government and, the armed forces which were directed to the Air Raid Centre (LSWK) we informed them of the attack on the Möhne dam and the possibility of an attack on the Eder Dam.

The Eder Dam is breached - Taken 18 May 1943. A photograph no one was allowed to see ... Until now. One can see the vast area breached.

The Eder Dam - Taken 19 May 1943. Again no one was allowed to see it. This photograph is the only one known of the west side of the Eder Dam and, was taken just two days after breaching. Note that the water level is under the lower edge of the breach. This was due to two pipes of some three metres in diameter, one at each end of the wall, through which water flowed into the turbines of the power stations.

The air situation was correctly interpreted as well as the importance of the (Eder) dam to the Kassel area and the city of Kassel. The wide-ranging consequences in the event of damage to the dam and the resulting flooding.

0201 0200 82683 (Usseln) aircraft noise low at 6-8

0202 0200 82811 (Winterberg) aircraft noise high at 3-1

0204 0203 92711 (Waldeck) 4 enemy aircraft- 4-engined retreating direction 9

0202 82683 (Usseln) aircraft noise low 4-7

0205 0201 82311 (Beckum) aircraft noise low 9-10

0205 92711 (Waldeck) 4-engined aircraft noise light beams over dam

0206 0206 Hs   (Henschel) Altenbauna in area 9 nothing to see (report)

0204 82724 (Fredeburg) aircraft noise high area 11

0204 82761 (Oberkirchen) aircraft noise high at 1-12

0207 Periodic report 19: aircraft 'lingering' in Marsberg - Reservoir area

0208 0206 82451 (Oberntudort) aircraft noise low at 3

0213 0208 82374 (Korbecke) 1 enemy aircraft 4-engined low at 4-10

0213 82353 (Wiegeringhausen) aircraft noise low 10-11, distant high (!)

0216 0215 82374 (Korbecke) aircraft noise high at 6-4

0218 Periodic report 20: aircraft from the Eder reservoir area retreating to NW

0223 0220 82683 (Usseln) aircraft noise medium height at 3, distant high

0225 0224 82663 (Rosenbeck) aircraft noise at 7

0226 0215 92711 (Waldeck) aircraft noise high at 9, distant high

0227 0222 82311 (Beckum) continuous aircraft noise medium height at 12-11

0229 0227 82874 (Battenberg) aircraft noise high at 3-2,

distant high

0235 Periodic report 21: One enemy aircraft circling in area Marburg/Lahn

0236 ADVICE FROM BAD WILDUNGEN. THE CENTRE AT MAUSER FACTORY AT WALDECK REPORTS 'AFFOLDERN IS UNDERWATER (FLOODED), HOUSES COLLAPSING.'

0242 Periodic report 22: THE EDER DAM HAS BEEN HIT

0258 Periodic report 23: 3 aircraft circling in area Dortmund-Munster various courses

0300 All clear given for Witzenhausen-Eschwege 0301 All clear given for railway group east 0308 Air raid warning lifted for Kassel

0311 Air raid warning for railway groups central and south lifted

0312 All clear given for Melsungen

0314 Periodic report 24: The air situation in our area has quietened down, west of Arnsberg-Munster little enemy activity

Note:

It is interesting to see that the Air Raid Warning Control Centre in Kassel which, made this report, did not receive the advice that the Eder Dam had been hit until 0242. At 0236 they received a report from the Mauser factory at Waldeck, which is at the Eder reservoir, that Affoldern was under water. This village is on the bank of the Eder river 4 kilometres down-stream. At 0218 Periodic report 20 states, 'enemy aircraft retreating to NW'

Possibly the centre did not believe the report of 0236 and 0242.

As the drama unfolded in the night sky above them, the residents of the nearby village of Affoldem took to the adjacent hills in order to escape the approaching death flood.

Under the command of Wing Commander Guy Gibson the bombers were circling in preparation for an attack against the unprotected Eder Dam.

Time and again the lead bomber circled the area around the dam, as if willing his bombers to create mass destruction ... This was Gibson's Lancaster and, it was picked-out by a young German housewife who, was one of the lucky ones that managed to find high ground before the dam burst.

She followed the deadly silhouette of Gibson's bomber ... and shivering with fright she uttered, 'Curse you, you evil Terror-Flieger, curse you. I, Frau Kloppman, curse you, lead Terror-Flieger, to crash and die a horrid death by fire, for you, are from the Teufel.'

She was frightened. She was mad, as would be anyone in that frightful situation, one that many British could relate to when they were on the receiving end of German bombs, or when the Americans were hit at Pearl Harbour and I have no doubt they also uttered a thousand curses. The night of 17 May was a nightmare for at that stage of the war, the German people were already poor and hungry. Now, what food and animals they had, had been destroyed in the death flood.

Eder Dam taken two days after breaching. And no one was allowed to see it. In foreground is a power station and another one far left adjacent to the dam wall. Some construction equipment can be seen on top of the dam wall behind the flagpole.

Hundreds of people experienced the nightmare wall of water that washed away their houses and property under the Eder Dam - the type of house in this area being Tudor style, substantial beams filled in with straw and plaster.

The day after the dams raid, Frau Kloppman's husband, Heinrich, came on leave to his home at Dornberg. At great risk to their lives, Heinrich Kloppman and his wife cycled to a spot, protected by bushes, overlooking the dam via Ippinghausen, Sachsenhausen and Werpe, some 35 kilometres. Here they took photographs using a Kodak 6 x 9mm camera.

They took a great risk taking the photographs for it was forbidden to take any photographs. And, at this period there were many guards at all key points. But as is always the case, that did not stop forbidden photographs from being taken, and, it did not stop Kloppman taking two sensational photographs - as we can now see.

The devastation. Kassel on 19 May 1943... thousands killed and missing. Another rare photograph shown here for the first time.

It did help greatly with Kloppman being in his Panzer uniform. And the vast destruction also helped, for the Flak Units had to detour via Dornberg due to the approach roads being washed away. The Kloppman's gave some schoolboys 50 pfennig for helping to carry their bicycles over the obstacles.

From the top of a hill they were able to see Affoldern, which was flooded.

Then came the difficult task in getting the film developed. A Kassel photographer refused outright to develop and print the film and quickly turned them away.

After Heinrich Kloppman had gone back to his unit, the 1st Panzer Division that, was then in occupied France; Frau Kloppman gave the film to a friend who in turn, took it to another friend who, worked at the IG Farben factory at Hoechst, near to Darmstadt. Relatives then brought the unique photographs and the negatives back to Frau Kloppman who immediately hid them away.

The official documents state that the raid on the Ruhr dams led to 1,294 deaths and that most of these were near the Möhne Dam, especially in the town of Neheim-Husten that suffered over 900. All were drowned. But unofficial figures say well over 5,000 were killed. There is no record of animal casualties for they were vast, too vast to assess.

Meanwhile, the curse and the photographs remained Frau Kloppman's secret.

Back in England, Frau Kloppman's curse was starting

to work ... saving Gibson for his special curse, for he was from the Teufel, the Devil. Thirty-five of the Dam Busters were killed in three nights within a month of Gibson being posted to Special Duties in August 1943.

The raid against the Ruhr dams had been a costly failure. Yes, the damage to power stations, factory buildings, houses, roads, bridges and to agriculture was enormous and wiped out complete families. But it was only done to smash the will of the German people, for Bomber Command made no attempt to stop the repair work on the dams.

So was Frau Kloppman right to curse the Terror-Fliegers? I'm sure many cursed them that night, but then we cursed the Germans as much. It is true the dam raid was more political, but also a wonderful propaganda and moral booster. There is no doubt that the dams raid was a truly daring and brave mission and it rightfully earned Gibson the Victoria Cross.

Many of the brave pilots who survived the dams raid, sadly died in the following two years. On the night of 19-20 September 1944 Wing Commander Guy Gibson volunteered to act as Master Bomber and, set course in his borrowed de Havilland Mosquito for Rheydt, just inside the German border.

Gibson left the target area ... but it seems that sadly it is almost as if that curse, that was given in the emotion of the time, was now to be played out. According to eyewitnesses, Gibson's Mosquito was seen to crash in flames near the town of Steenbergen-en-Kruisland in Holland.

Back at RAF Scampton, the King bends over the target photographs while Gibson looks on.

A ball of flame ... just as the curse stated. And for many years, the crash was not identified ... forgotten.

In early 1987, Frau Kloppman let the sensational photographs, which she and her husband took in May 1943, see the light of day and, I was first to have a copy and, the documents with the photographs.

I know that there may well have been many curses from both friend and foe as emotions are at their highest and the ordinary person in the middle of all this terror finds themselves so helpless. And I cannot say whether Frau Kloppman ever knew how Gibson died, but what is fact, is the photographs and indeed the many strange and un-answered things that have surrounded this brave and audacious mission.

From the beginning with the mystery of how Nigger

died, right through to the mystery around Wing Commander Guy Gibson's death ... 'seen to crash to the ground in a ball of flame,' said eye witnessed accounts of Gibson's crash ... consumed by fire. There has always been something strange about this mission, with its many dark secrets. Does the answer lie back in Lincolnshire? Yes. Lincolnshire holds more secrets and mysteries than people suspect or realize.

Frau Kloppman's curse was one of many by ordinary people, given in the heat of emotion and so cannot be really looked on as being the cause for the strange events that surround this mission, for after all Nigger had already been mysteriously killed. But was a curse given by someone or something much closer to home? Maybe from quarters that would never have been suspected?

Now that the photographs have come to light and, the curse on those Terror-Fliegers that launched the death flood on so many men, women, children and animals, also made known, it does show how cruel war is, and why we have so many restless Spirits, wanting us to know the truth that others for what ever reason have tried to hide or destroy.

Since the above was researched I have solved the mystery of Wing Commander Gibson's demise; and how and why Nigger was killed. I explain all in my new book **Ghost Stations™** Mysteries.

THE PHANTOMS OF TINTWHISTLE KNARRS

In February 1995 I received a very interesting letter from Alan Jones of Stalybridge in Cheshire. It was an interesting letter for many reasons: one, it supported previous material in **Ghost Stations™** and is as follows: "In your last book you have a story concerning the Defiant night fighter which crashed on Near Bleaklow Stones near Woodhead," he said "I once met the two young men who say they saw a ghost at the site and as far as I know they are sensible lads." and Alan Jones added: "As for myself, I have spent the last thirty years visiting over fifty crash sites in the Peak District, including the Defiant, on many occasions. I have to say that even in dense misty conditions I have never experienced anything supernatural.

"The heaviest loss of life occurred on a B29 crash at Shelf Stones just outside Glossops, where thirteen men died. My friends and I have spent hours at this site, often in dense low cloud but, have never seen anything out of the ordinary. This brings me to the reason for contacting you."

And it is a very interesting ghostly reason, as you will now find out. On his walks, Alan is usually accompanied by his close friend, Jim Chatterton, aged seventy-three, of Tintwhistle. Jim spends a lot of time on a nearby hill called Tintwhistle Knarrs where five aircraft have crashed. These are namely a Lancaster bomber, a Lockheed Lightning and three Hurricanes;

from all these crashes there were no survivors. The three Hurricanes crashed in formation in low cloud and Jim has combed the hillside with his metal detector, recovering small scraps of aircraft and, in one instance, the back of a watch. Despite visiting these crash sites nearly every week in the summer months, he also has seen nothing ghostly; that is, until one bright sunny day in 1994.

On this particular day Jim had climbed the hill via the Hurricanes crash site, then made his way to the Lockheed Lightning. Finding nothing of interest, he started back home, stopping for a few minutes at the Lancaster site on the brow of the hill. Here again, his search proved fruitless.

It was a perfect still, sunny, cloudless day and after admiring the view, he started down the moor towards his home in Tintwhistle, a distance around two miles. About half way down the moor the ground levels out with a gully on the right of the path and slightly rising ground on the left. Here, as he glanced to his left, he saw the sun reflecting on what he took to be the square windows of a Jeep or Land Rover, beside which he saw the figure of a man. Thinking it was a Range Warden, he realized his metal detector, which he usually carried in a cover, was still open to view and, as he did not want any trouble, he thought it best to cover it up.

Jim turned away from the man to hide his intentions and when he looked back again the Jeep and figure of the man were gone … vanished into thin air.

When asked how far away he was from the man and the jeep, Jim replied:

"No more than fifty yards." Alan Jones has known Jim Chatterton for thirty years: "He is a down to earth sensible man, having spent most of his life on the local moors involved with shooting and aviation archaeology," he said. And he added: "We can't explain this phenomenon."

It is very strange and I cannot offer any logical explanation. It is a known fact that eleven men died on Tintwhistle Knarrs and, a well known local farmer died under his tractor but, none were at the spot where Jim Chatterton saw the man and jeep on a clear sunny day.

When asked what he made of the ghostly sighting, Alan Jones replied: "I have heard tales from other enthusiasts who visit the Peak District crash sites; but I tend to treat them with a pinch of salt. Often the cries of moor land birds or sheep sound very much like human voices. I have experienced this on several occasions, also many weird shapes are conjured up by the swirling mists; putting the two together can account for many ghostly encounters I'm sure; but in Jim's case it was a perfect afternoon and I know Jim. He's not a liar so what could it have been?"

GHOST WATCH 1987

The now abandoned runway at RAF Fiskerton

On Saturday, 31st October 1987, Radio Lincolnshire linked up with three East Midlands BBC Local Radio Stations; for a three-hour programme called Ghost Watch, from ten o'clock on the Saturday night until one o'clock the following morning.

Dennis McCarthy hosted the programme from the supposedly haunted cellar in the Hippo Club, Bridlesmithgate, Nottingham. From the start, Dennis did make it clear that there were no gimmicky voices and that the programme was live. The three-selected ... Reputedly haunted sites ... were the Hippo Club in

Nottingham, the Malt Shovel in Derby, and an airfield in Lincolnshire. As a military historian and former Royal Air Force Police Special Security (Atomic & Chemical Weapons) SS, I was the expert in Lincolnshire.

Just before ten o'clock in the evening, it was announced that it was time to join Dennis McCarthy and East Midlands Ghost Watch. We now join the programme ... Ghost Watch.

Dennis McCarthy: "Welcome to Ghost Watch in the East Midlands, perhaps for the first time BBC Radio is covering a large part of England in a live programme looking for a ghost. This programme is not intended to raise any spirit or ghost - we are not going to have a séance - in fact I am sure that everyone taking part would be against anyone organizing a séance or dabbling with the supernatural. To do that is dangerous. But to talk about the subject might be healthy and might even get rid of some of the fears, behind ghosts, because there are very few reports anywhere of any ghosts doing any physical harm to anyone. We cover the East Midlands in this programme, Leicestershire, Derbyshire, Lincolnshire and Nottinghamshire."

Dennis McCarthy then invited listeners to phone in with their ghost stories and went on to say that the East Midlands is a rich area for ghosts. The programme came from the cellar of the Hippo Club, where at various times, ghosts have been seen in period costume; it is in fact close to a civil war battle area and, one of the sightings reported was of a figure in a Cavalier uniform. Many strange happenings have been recorded at the

Hippo, which has been reputed to be haunted for a long, long time. With Dennis McCarthy in the cellar was an unusual panel of experts, Lee Lacy, a Nottingham Medium; Kris Sky, a White Witch; Diane Blatherwick, a Psychic Investigator and Cannon John Finnay, an advisor in Evangelism in the diocese of Southwell.

The haunted location in Lincolnshire was the old wartime airfield of RAF Fiskerton. For security reasons the location was not announced over the air at the start of the programme. Radio Lincolnshire had, in fact, received a couple of threatening calls. So it was decided to keep the location secret. However, many people still turned up on the night ... after working out the location from my books.

I selected the old Fiskerton airfield (any would have done), but this gave good reception with having to work from a mobile car. During the war, the airfield had two main squadrons, Nos. 49 and 576. The latter flew 2,788 operational sorties and lost 67 aircraft. Also, Fiskerton was one of 15 airfields equipped with FIDO - Fog Investigation Dispersal Operation. Many ghostly happenings stemmed from the airfield. Norman Pepper was learning to drive on the old runways when suddenly a World War Two Jeep swept past with its cargo of ghostly aircrew. The old control tower was haunted; and the Royal Observer Corps building is haunted ... so an obvious choice.

The Memorial that now stands at RAF Fiskerton (it was not there at the time we did Ghost Watch in 1987)

The old wartime runway at Fiskerton in Lincolnshire, where now only the Ghost Squadrons are airborne.

With the Radio Lincolnshire radio car was Andy Smith, the reporter, who opened our location.

Andy Smith: "Yes Dennis it's very bleak here, the cloud cover is very low, mist around everywhere. Its damp … horrible underfoot … just listen to this having to tread through here. But so far nothing has happened. I will just describe where I am as you say. I am in the middle of an airfield, way over the other side, I guess about 300 to 400 yards there is a dim light where it is rumoured that perhaps a jeep … an old RAF jeep may suddenly come across the airfield and pass by the radio car which has its mast firmly up in the air ...very obvious target. To one other side . . . lights glittering in the distance if I look in another totally different direction, a few trees, again visibility is very bad so you could say that we have got the right eerie atmosphere for some quite interesting activities to happen on Halloween night. Now I have a few guests with me here, who will be analysing any suspected ghost or psychic powers that might suddenly appear.

"We have Bruce Barrymore Halpenny, the author and RAF Ghost Expert and also John Turner, and he is secretary of the Lincolnshire Psychic Society.

Andy Smith: "Now I have to admit John that I have never seen a ghost and I have never been involved in any sort of psychic powers at all so I am really a disbeliever but do you think you can convince me otherwise?"

John Turner: "Well, I just hope that something happens ... something decides to manifest so that you will be convinced but of course, obviously without it, I don't think you are going to be."

As a medium, John Turner said that he would sense it first probably before we would see it "In fact, you may not even see it," he said. As stated in **Ghost Stations™,** many mediums have a Red Indian Spirit Guide and John tells me that the name of his spirit guide is Running Bear. I am informed that he was the son of a Cherokee Indian Chief and he lived from 1770 to 1792. He died from a chest infection. And John added: "He was a full blooded Cherokee Indian."

After the initial introduction, Andy Smith passed back to Dennis McCarthy and it was interesting to hear him say: "I am very interested in haunted airfields or the possibility of haunted airfields my own theory about it is, that an airfield, particularly a wartime airfield is a very emotive place full of emotion. The men during wartime would make a flight and it was always said that after one flight over enemy territory they were living on borrowed time so their emotions would really be very strong. Do you think this might well create the environment ... Lee Lacy ... for a haunted airfield?

Lee Lacy answered that it could be and, he did say that he had not experienced a haunted airfield. He then said that whilst in the army, at a depot in Northamptonshire, men did report seeing a headless ghost on the railway lines. He explained that it was a worker who had had an accident and been decapitated by a railway carriage. Lee Lacey went on to say that he had a case about a gentleman, who reported in about an airman, who was walking back one night, after a night flight and, seeing an officer, saluted him but when he got back he found out that his plane had come down and that he had died a few hours before. Lacey said he could not explain it: "I would say that it could be that what he was sensing, he was maybe a little bit more psychic than he thought, he was sensing he was seeing a spirit ... a spirit ... ghost ... maybe different thing."

The third Ghost Watch location was in the reputed haunted cellar of the Malt Shovel Public House, in Shardlow, which is very close to the River Trent and Mersey Canal. The ghost there is Humphrey and legend has it that it is the ghost of a tramp, who was reputedly drowned, in a vat, by a foreman of the Malting, way back in the 1700's. The public house was built in 1799 but the ghost did not appear until in the early 1960s after major alterations had been carried out. A young man working on the new alterations first saw the ghost and, the landlord at that time, Peter Harrison, had seen it. He was in the cellar at the time and he thought it was a customer … he asked if he could help and with that it vanished before his eyes. The landlord's wife had also seen the ghost … in fact she was woken at about one o'clock in the morning with a voice calling her name . . . she awoke to see a shape looming over the bed. The dog that usually sleeps in the bedroom had gone. At the time there were workmen working and staying overnight. And, legend has it that the ghost only appears when alterations are being done.

Dennis McCarthy did ask Canon Finnay if it was right to do this programme, for he did say that they had been criticized for doing it. Canon Finnay did say that there were dangers in ghost hunting. Dennis then asked him the 64,000 dollar question … "Are there Ghosts?"

Canon Finnay: "There are many odd things that happen whether there are ghosts I wouldn't want to ask what a ghost is to be frank. For more than things being seen are things being felt or heard than an actual figure

146

of a man wandering round the tower with his head under his arm is a very, very rare beast indeed and to be frank, I have never come across anything of that kind."

"There is no classic location for sighting a ghost and there certainly isn't a rule which says that sightings are always for example at night and in deserted houses," said Dennis "individuals reporting encounters with what they believe spiritual ghosts in a host of situations."

Dennis then gave an example of two ladies who saw a ghost in a supermarket in Berwick-upon- Tweed . . . "It was just a black outline shaped like a man but no bottom half to it just a black shape, which then disappeared," said one of the ladies. The lights were full on in the supermarket so it was not a lighting problem and there was nothing that could have cast a shadow like that. Both ladies saw it. The manager, said: "By the looks of her she did see something for she was as white as a sheet."

Armed with the possibility that the supermarket might be haunted, the manager investigated it further. A local historian then informed him that years ago, the supermarket area used to be a public hanging yard. "You hear of mediums and so forth seeing things, I'm beginning to go along with it now," said the supermarket manager.

So with the scene set and, after further stories from listeners, Dennis came back to the Lincolnshire location . . . my location.

Dennis McCarthy: "We are going back ... I think, to our airfield somewhere in Lincolnshire and I rather think that our reporter there has got another guest,"

Andy Smith: "Indeed we have Dennis . . . not very haunted here at the moment but things could change. My guest is Bruce Barrymore Halpenny; he is the author and RAF Ghost Expert ...so reveal all about this airfield . . . is it really haunted?"

BBH: "Well yes, I think every airfield is actually. There was so much tragedy that took place during the war years, when we look back Bomber Command alone lost over 55,000 aircrew, they were killed in the air and have no known graves ... so there are a lot of earth bound spirits, if you want to say, that are still on the airfields. So much tragedy took place and every airfield has its ghosts, some more than others.

"There has been many sightings here, most of the buildings are now demolished. The control tower, when it was here, had many, many sightings, and often sounds were heard in the old building. On the airfield quite recently there have been sightings such as the jeep that you mentioned previously . . . there are also noises that most of the time sound like a Merlin engine; which have been heard many times ... in the still of an evening when there is no breeze. So yes, very, very haunted."

Andy Smith: "Now you have checked through all these facts thoroughly; do you think that . . . er . . . there is a pattern to the ... the evidence that comes up from time to time?"

BBH: "The evidence that is there . . . I do not think any of them are out to cause mischief. They are there to draw attention to themselves. There is this earthbound spirit and this is what it is all about. It is not always necessary to see the spirit or ghost or whatever; but the presence is there."

"Bruce this is Dennis can you hear me"

BBH: "Yes, very clear"

Dennis McCarthy: "You made a most interesting recording on a haunted airfield and we have the recording standing by, I would like you to tell us where it is and, introduce the recording so that we can hear it and get a proper explanation from you."

BBH: "Yes, this was done at Bircham Newton in the squash court under supervised conditions ... a lot of people were there, there was no jiggery pokery, I would not be interested to do that, that sort of thing could easily be arranged, but this tape is perfectly true and genuine. The tape was set up and there were two or three recordings made, many times they did not work. This particular tape was set up and the people were very, very frightened and did not stay in the squash court ... they switched it on and came out and we now hear the tape that I have."

BBH: The chilling tape was then played over the airwaves; and the Ghost Watch programme listeners heard the unearthly noises, just like people working in a wartime hangar. I then went on to explain that only the tape-recorder picked up those noises and no one there, that night heard them ... no aircraft were in the area and, let us remember it was recorded in a squash court not in a hangar. There were **no** metallic objects in the squash court. With my second Special Ghost book well on the way and Time Zone theory I did not mention that for I was still working on it. But, it is clear that the tape recorder had picked up sounds from the past. Dennis McCarthy came back to say that medium Lee Lacey wanted a word with me.

Lee Lacey: "There are couple of points. The thing that is disturbing me a little bit about this, Dennis, is that the implication is that all these things are supernatural noises and things ... it sounded like old beer crates rolling around to me ... er ... but ... the thing that bothers me is the statement earlier that all airfields are haunted ... which is the biggest rubbish ... absolute rubbish ... where any dramatic event has been ... where there has been murders ... where there has been people that have ... err ... high tensions and things that have got up they leave what I like to call a tape-recorder effect ... they leave implanted something that sensitive people can pick up and it doesn't necessarily mean to say that there is a ghost there ... and the implication is ... or what I was getting the impression ... was ... you know ... that ... if they are not careful every airfield tomorrow they will have people going out ghost hunting ... which would be silly and a bit disastrous."

Dennis McCarthy: "Yes ... and the Reverend John Finnay ... er ... I believe ... you want to come in on that one."

Canon John Finnay: "Yes, err … I used to be in the Air Force and I can remember going out when I was night flying and, it is a very, very . . . eerie feeling . . . dim red lights . . . dim blue lights . . . of the runway and so forth … err … a little bit of early morning mist swirling around and you can see almost anything. At the same time, one has to remember that from that those airfields in some cases … obviously … erm … people did take off and didn't come back; and there is those sorts of memories at the back of many people's minds I think and putting those two together the slight eerie feel which was a very understandable thing; erm in that sort of area and plus the memories and you very, very quickly begin to get the sort of stories. And, like Lee, I felt very unhappy about the idea that every airfield was haunted."

Dennis McCarthy: "But … but let's get back to Bruce Halpenny. Because to be fair to Bruce, Bruce you have had a lot of stories given to you … by many, many people".

BBH: "Oh yes, and thoroughly researched, I mean Lord Balfour of Inchrye, who is 90 tomorrow, the Montrose Ghost. All the people are Air Vice Marshals, Squadron Leaders with absolutely nothing to gain. If you would just tell me an airfield where no tragedy took place then I might believe you.

Dennis McCarthy: "Are you really saying Bruce, that there is a ghost on every airfield"

BBH: "I am saying there is a presence . . . or a ghost. It doesn't mean to say that you see a ghost … people have seen half ghosts … they have felt things, they have heard thing. Being former Provost, I then went on to say that on just about all the airfields there were sections, which the police dogs would not walk across. And I repeated for them to name me an airfield where no tragedy took place from the so-called experts, Lee Lacey and Canon John Finnay … it came down to definition. As stated in **Ghost Stations ™** in many cases it all comes down to Religion . . . with a capital **R**. What is definition? For the so-called experts, the dictionary defines definition - 'to determine, bring to an end' - but for Roman Catholicism, it means: 'an official ecclesiastical statement concerning a matter of faith or of morals as pertaining to faith.' So we are back to religion where the supernatural started in the first place.

"So Canon John Finnay has nothing to write home about. Let him tell me why. There are so many Christian ghosts and ghosts of monks and nuns . . . all back to religion. On the Ghost Watch programme, Dennis read out stories about Hardwick Hall, which was built in Elizabethan times. In 1976, a couple were driving through Hardwick Park when they saw the figure of a hooded monk in their headlights. The monk wore a black habit and they said his face was brilliant white. Also, a couple in another car and two policemen had seen the ghostly hooded monk. So why all these Christian ghosts, have they no God? Are they Evil? According to Canon Finnay . . . Yes."

After a tour round the other locations, and hearing of listeners ghost stories, Dennis came back to Lincolnshire.

Dennis McCarthy: "Now we are going to go back to Lincolnshire . . . an airfield somewhere in Lincolnshire with our reporter, Andy Smith."

Andy Smith: "And you thought it was cold, Dennis, its freezing here ... there are five of us now and we are all huddled fairly close together and we do have a woman with us now, so things have certainly improved ... not that close but people are now saying – where's the drinks cabinet, where's the whisky, we've got to warm ourselves up somehow - Still no sightings here at all I am afraid. But as we were talking earlier, Bruce Halpenny has written the book about ghosts and, in particular, was talking about RAF Hemswell and the book prompted Dave and Penny Kitchen, of Heighington, near Lincoln, and Penny is with me at the moment. Take us back to that day in May what happened?"

Penny Kitchen: "Well, my husband received the book for Christmas and he read some of the stories to me and the children and we found them quite evocative although I must admit I was quite sceptical but as the weather got better we decided well, there was nothing to lose we would go and see if there was anything to be seen. We drove up past the hangars to the main runway and my husband and the children got out. I was still so sceptical I sat there and they walked off into the distance then, suddenly, I thought I heard a dog panting and just looked round but there was nothing, so I dismissed it until about two minutes later I heard it again and there was nothing there. It was just like a dog panting."

Andy Smith: "Then in the distance - the disused hangar and more eerie goings on?"

Penny Kitchen: "Yes - they came back to the car and I told them what I heard and this really set the atmosphere I think we were prepared for anything then. We turned round and drove up towards the hangar and there was a light; well you could just see a light through the chinks at the top of the hangar and so we were quite excited and we stopped the car and looked and there definitely were lights."

Andy Smith: "Now, did you tell your friends about this?"

Penny Kitchen: "Yes, we are both teachers and we told our friends at school and they thought it was hilarious but they did agree to come and have a look. So we all set off one night and walked around the hangar, we were quite a lot braver because there was a lot of us and we did get out of the car."

Andy Smith: "Did the dog reappear?"

Penny Kitchen: "No. No … the dog has never reappeared just the lights. There was nothing to do; we had seen them so we went off home. But I did write to the people who used the hangars as a grain store and they wrote back to say that they had had trouble with the lights, they couldn't switch them off. Well, that seemed a reasonable explanation but it also seemed a coincidence that it should be that hangar, the one that we had read about in the book."

Andy Smith: "You are obviously quite happy to talk about that sort of experience and if I can just bring John Turner in who is the secretary of the Lincolnshire Psychic Society. Penny obviously, is quite happy to talk about that, but not many people; perhaps some people don't want to admit they may have seen a ghost."

John Turner: "No a lot of people won't admit it ... er ... mainly because they are frightened of people saying that; er . . . there is something wrong with them, er . . . being called nut cases and things like that. And they tend to bottle it up inside themselves."

Andy Smith: "O.K. John and quickly to Bruce ... you're the author of the book so how do you interpret Penny's recollection."

BBH: "Well, it is as I have said earlier this evening that every airfield is haunted, you do not necessarily have to see a ghost as this lady has shown this evening. She heard a dog panting and there wasn't a dog there, the lights were flashing in the hangar and this is what I said. Every airfield."

Dennis McCarthy: "Can I; can I . . . just butt in here, Bruce, for I want you to hang on and hear a call that we have got coming through from a former Duty Engineer at RAF Syerston, Val Watmo from Bottesford ... Val"

Val Watmo: "Yes. Good Evening, Dennis, er, going back in 1959, I think it was late one night I was on duty. I was called out to one of the hangars because the hangar lights were going on and off, on and off. So all the RAF Police and the guard and the likes thought . . . hello . . . we have got an erk in here whose been out on the drink and having some fun. So the hangar was duly surrounded by the police and police dogs and we went in through the fire door, which are doors in the centre of the hangar not the big ones at each end. We had got two Alsatians, the doors opened and the lights were certainly going on and off ... the dogs could not be dragged in; no way would they go near the fire doors . . . er . . . and they were used to going in the hangars. They used to come in normally, quite often.

"We appeared in the hangar; er . . . on the right hand side where the main contactor was, which was used to switch on the power . . . on and off . . . when the lights went out you could see a human side glow that is the only way I can describe it ... it wasn't the ... You couldn't pick a person out you could certainly pick out a glow of somebody there or something there, so we decided that ... we weren't going to hang about, it certainly wasn't a person because when the lights came on there was nothing to be seen, so there was nobody lurking there. We closed the hangar doors very quickly . . . or the fire doors very quickly . . . which were steel doors . . . locked them up and, next morning, nobody went in there until the padre had been in. And he went into the hangar and eventually came out again and it was reported that an airman who had been killed or apparently been killed on the airfield, was responsible now, I don't know, I wasn't on duty in the morning; but ... er, that is a story that goes. And talking of airfields, one other place that is of interest near RAF Newton is Oakfield Lane, which runs from the A52 … top of the A52 at Saxondale across to Shellford Road; now that's often used by courting couples. There has been a lot of reports. Oh, I've never seen this one but regularly reported that ghostly sightings have been seen on this road. So there's a couple of things for you."

Dennis McCarthy: "Thank you very much indeed Bruce. Any comment on that?"

BBH: "No, it is just something that bears out everything that I have written in my books and said previously."

Dennis McCarthy: "What about RAF Syerston, have you any reports in your book about that one?"

"No…but I have many files of ones from there, some that I am going to use in my new book that comes out next year."

Dennis McCarthy: "Andy, you were talking about the temperature on that Lincolnshire Airfield…you feeling cold?"

Andy Smith: "I think the word is desperate."

Dennis McCarthy: "Well, you see some strange things have happened here in the cellar because the . . . the temperature gauge isn't making sense at all; it is going up and down and a few minutes ago, it dropped four degrees."

Andy Smith: "I think the same problem is happening here because our mast on the Radio Car is obviously feeling the cold, it keeps; er … retracting into itself to keep warm I think."

After more listeners' stories, Dennis comes back to us at the Lincolnshire location:

Dennis McCarthy: "We are now going to go to our airfield somewhere in Lincolnshire and our reporter, Andy Smith.

Andy Smith: "Sorry Dennis you just; erm . . . caught me like David Dimbleby; eating a mouthful of nosh when you came over to me there. But we have been having a discussion, since our last report and it is rather strange because although I didn't sense something happening John Turner of the Lincolnshire Psychic Research Group said something definitely happened. So, John I think . . . just explain what happened."

John Turner: "Well, I saw your reaction first because you turned and looked behind you ... as you had the feeling that there was something there; and at the same time, I felt something pass us very, very quickly from left to right."

Andy Smith: "Can you describe what it was?"

John Turner: "No, I can't. It passed so fast I just didn't have a chance to see what it was."

Andy Smith: "Can you try and sort of work out what this might indicate?"

John Turner: "Er ... whether it was connected with the airfield I don't know, all I can say is there was something definitely there that passed very quickly."

Andy Smith: "But as I didn't see it why should I believe it?"

John Turner: "Well, you did look round, as if you had the feeling there was someone behind you and I noticed you looking round as it happened."

Andy Smith: "Now, if you are listening at home you might be thinking what a load of old rubbish; don't believe it but our other expert also felt the same thing, Bruce Halpenny, how would you interpret it?"

BBH: "Yes there was, we were expecting to see something when you say, I didn't see anything why should I believe it. The thing is you don't have to see it, as I said previously and you felt something. There was a strange draught, it was going from left to right … we all looked in the same direction but by this time, it had passed over the vehicle. We were all pre-occupied with something else."

Andy Smith: "Now, at the time of our last broadcast, there was no traffic going past at all so it is obviously not headlights but the fact we are on a disused airfield and you were saying, Bruce that there are earth spirits in disused airfields; wherever they are … are we perhaps infringing on their ground. How would you interpret?"

BBH: "Yes, this is what I should say; that you are definitely infringing on their ground. Yes."

Andy Smith: "And what about John?"

John Turner: "Yes I agree completely; you see, this is their home to them. It is their home and we are strangers in their home."

Andy Smith: "Well I wonder if anyone else saw it. We ask the questions. Dennis, any ideas at all?"

Dennis McCarthy: "Well if anybody would like to ring us on Nottingham 343434 we would be glad to put them on the air Andy."

Andy Smith: "O.K ... but at the moment it's all quiet. The lights over the other side of the airfield have all gone out so we're certainly almost the only civilization on here."

After stories from the other locations and stories from listeners. Dennis McCarthy returned to us in Lincolnshire.

Dennis McCarthy: "We are now going over to Lincolnshire to an airfield somewhere in Lincolnshire and with our radio car ... Andy Smith ... Andy."

Andy Smith: "Yes. Hello again Dennis I think at this point we can ... we can reveal the location and to do that for me is Bruce Barrymore Halpenny who is the author and RAF Ghost Expert ... where are we?"

BBH: "We are at a disused airfield just outside of Lincoln at the old RAF Fiskerton airfield."

Andy Smith: "Now we have been talking about its history throughout the evening, during the last few minutes, a group has tracked down our location, come onto the airfield and has said there were a few flashes and possibly bangs from the area, which we think is the Observation Corps."

BBH: "That's right, which is a purpose built site that they have on the other section of the airfield, one of the old dispersal pans."

Andy Smith: "Now there have been some strange sightings there as well haven't there?"

160

BBH: "Yes, they've had two or three that have been substantiated. A Phantom Officer has been seen in the complex but, of course, owing to security reasons it is not possible to substantiate this and, of course, naturally these have been denied but they are by people involved in the complex and the sightings have been positive."

Andy Smith: "Why do you think that the Ministry of Defence is so coy about it and doesn't really want to be drawn into the issue?

BBH: "It's just something they cannot admit to actually."

Andy Smith: "Let's have a quick chat with John Turner of the Lincolnshire Psychic Research Group, now that we have revealed the location, what sort of stories would you like to bring out as we draw towards the close of our Lincolnshire Ghost Watch?"

John Turner: "Well, I personally had one very interesting experience, I was going to bed very late one night, it was about half-past two in the morning and myself and my wife had just got into bed and we heard aircraft engines. Now once you heard a Merlin engine you never forget it and this was a Merlin engine and, it was coming closer and closer and getting louder and louder. And I was quite convinced that in actual fact, it was going to crash into the house. It was obvious, it was getting lower as it got nearer and then it seemed to just to pass just over the roof but then suddenly the noise of the engines just cut out. They didn't fade, they just stopped completely. And my first reaction was, oh its crashed. But there was nothing to be found and later on, I mentioned this to someone, who had been in the Home Guard at the time, during the war and he remembered actually being called out to guard a crashed aircraft which had crashed in a field only about a hundred yards from the house."

Andy Smith: "Now, you heard the engine but did anybody else hear it?"

John Turner: "Well, my wife did, I mean we both heard it quite clear; er … to be quite honest; we were scared to start with because we were convinced it was going to crash into the house, it was that low."

Andy Smith: "Now we were talking about sensing that psychic powers are in evidence, is it just yourself and your wife who are able to sense this engine going across or were various people around your locality saying we heard it as well."

John Turner: "Well we never heard of anyone else … erm … it was as far as I know just the two of us."

Andy Smith: "I just quickly want to bring in what we've been talking about when we haven't been on the air about it not being a gift, that you can sense these powers. How would you describe it?"

John Turner: "It's not a gift … erm … everyone has the ability, if they're prepared to develop it. You have got to go about developing it and you must do it under supervision as well."

Andy Smith: "Obviously brings us round to what Dennis was saying about you mustn't dabble in the supernatural."

John Turner: "Oh no ... no. Definitely not, it can be dangerous to dabble; you must do it under supervision. That supervision of another medium."

Andy Smith: "Well, that's the position so far on the Fiskerton Airstrip in Lincolnshire, hardly any lights on at all now ... the mist is still all around the car, but no more activity, we'll bring you up to date on that flash that we told you about just after eleven o'clock, see if we can think of any possible reason, it might even happen again, we don't know, we've still got twenty minutes to go, but that's it from Lincolnshire Ghost Watch at the moment."

Dennis then gives stories about haunted mines from the area and read out a story from the Nottingham Evening Post, dated Thursday, 8th October 1987. And the ghosts in the theatre and about a theatre ghost buster who was the only one to mention goulie on the programme and his definition of a ghost was: "Well ghosts ... apparitions ... whatever you want to call them are basically very, very basically the principle is its almost like photography if you like, a negative imprint that's left on the earth's atmosphere by somebody whose passed away but really didn't want to go; that really wanted to linger in the place where they were most happy and very simply that's what a ghost is." Interesting. Dennis then came back for the close of the programme.

Andy Smith: "Yes ... and its still very cold here. I must admit I'm glad we've come to the end of our three hours of watching and it has been eventful because as we mentioned earlier just after eleven o'clock, there was that flash and, just to briefly recap, here's John Turner of the Lincolnshire Psychic Research Group."

John Turner: "Yes, this was something that went past very, very fast I didn't have a chance to see what it was. We were all aware of it, which I'm rather glad that it's not just me aware of it. As I say, we were all aware of it, it was too fast. But whilst I've been here tonight; a name keeps coming back to me and the name is Travers; and the rank of Wing Commander. Now I've told that to Bruce and I understand that he will look into it."

Andy Smith: "Is there any reason why this should suddenly just come to you?"

John Turner: "No ... none what I know of."

Andy Smith: "Not connected with this flash perhaps."

John Turner: "Er no. This has come since it's just the name Travers and the rank of Wing Commander."

Andy Smith: "Well, lets go to Bruce Barrymore Halpenny, the author and RAF Ghost Expert. What do you make of that?"

BBH: "What I will do now is check the files to see if there is anyone by that name that has been on the airfield when it was operational."

Andy Smith: "Are you hopeful that something will come from this, because I know you have had a lot of people that's told you lots of information; and in most cases, you have been able to prove it."

BBH: "That is right, it has been most rewarding actually. And it has been very nice to know that we have not upset anyone."

Andy Smith: "Now we've spent three hours here ... there was that flash; are you disappointed that there wasn't something a bit more concrete coming out across the airfield?"

BBH: "Well, it is not a matter of being disappointed, it is a matter of just coming here. It is impossible to come and expect to see or feel something."

Dennis McCarthy: "Andy ... thank you very much indeed and will you thank your guests there for braving the elements ... I think we could say tonight."

That brought to an end the Ghost Watch programme. So let us sum-up the outcome of it all. After having listened to all the waffle from the experts in Nottingham, I was very pleased that I had not put forward my theory of a Time Zone. Let us remember, they claim to be the experts. Lee Lacey talked about good and bad spirits. Diane Blatherwick said about The Power of Suggestion. Canon John Finnay rambled on about people wanting to contact a consultant like himself, and said there are three classes of power. There is the power of God and of Goodness; there is the Human Power ... we can hate, we can love and so on; and there is also the power of Evil. From the experts, you will note, no mention of religion, and yet often it all comes down to religion. Canon Finnay said with suicides, all are evil. So Dr. Gareth Bennett, the churchman who committed suicide was evil; according to Canon Finnay, but the newspapers said: Death of a Christian. So the church ought to be asking itself a few questions.

Dennis McCarthy asked Diane Blatherwick a very good question, and that was: "Why are ghosts so reluctant to make themselves known when we have such a set up as we have here tonight - micro phones, cameras and investigators - why won't the ghost appear?"

"Well, I think it is as Lee Lacey said, there is too much going on," replied Diane Blatherwick. "But why won't they show themselves? Why are they so reluctant?" asked Dennis. "I don't know," she said "Maybe they will." Well, they never did.

At the Derbyshire location. No. "Nothing unusual happened at all," said reporter Gary Andrews.

At the Nottingham location; no logical explanation for the drop in temperature. For the drop in the temperature, Lee Lacey said he was aware of a presence. "Only an awareness I didn't see a presence standing behind your producer in that corner," he quickly added. Lacey also talked about a mirror image ... whatever that is ... and a tape-recorder effect gets left, imprinted in the bricks. Confused? Well I was. What about people who were buried in open ground, no tell tale bricks to tell the dastardly deed. And what of buildings that are knocked down and rebuilt, yet a ghost still walks the original paths of the original building ... the original bricks have all been removed. And what of phantom aircraft seen and heard … where were the bricks … and so the list can go on and on. Is it all done with mirrors?

With the drop in the temperature, Canon Finnay was asked if there was anything. He then rambled on … remember, he is a man of God … that where there have been violent incidents, suicides and such like, there is a feeling of disease, Till in the name of Christ they are told to get lost' … 'Get Lost!' … I ask you, and what feeling of disease? Dennis McCarthy then asked Canon Finnay: "Does that assume that everything there, is Evil?" – "Yes," replied Canon Finnay.

My answer to that is that that is all total bunkum … it is all back to religion. If you cannot understand it, it must be evil say the Christians, or it's down to the personal whim or prejudices of someone who uses religion as a tool to backup their biased ignorant beliefs that it's evil. But that is not the case; it does not have to be evil … only religion made it evil, which begs the question, who really is evil?

As for the cases of ghosts, phantoms, spirits etc, no two cases are the same … history, violence or cause of death, emotional feelings, trauma, a culmination of circumstances and so the list can go on. This is where serious research is needed for each and every case, not a "one explanation fits all", that so called experts try to claim.

So the outcome of it all proves one thing … what I say in **Ghost Stations™** is right.

OFFICIAL MYTHOLOGY

Because so many aircrew met violent deaths and, have no known graves this gave rise to a legend that the old abandoned airfields are haunted. Official Mythology has fuelled this belief, knowing there is a very strong emotional element of the casualties involved. Families and relatives of those who were killed or maimed are understandably acutely distressed on learning the real details of the wartime action, which bereaved them and changed their lives. They much prefer to cling to the belief, which authority readily offers, that it was part of a worthwhile cause and leave it at that. And so takes over Official Mythology.

"I now find it difficult, with the passage of time and consequent changing social issues and standards of values, to look back on the war years as something which really happened. In so many ways it all belongs to another world, a world long gone, which bears little relation to our own of today. And yet, in the course of just a few hours in that control tower with its contents, among people who were interested and were there to discuss their interest, so much came alive again which usually lies at the back of one's mind and yet somehow lies there uneasily" said Harry Wilson.

Harry was ex-aircrew and had attended one of my lectures and he was not on his own with his feelings. If, at the distance of some 50 years from the actual events, one tries to seek a balanced view of the role of the RAF in wartime Britain and approaches the matter with the assumption that the necessary information by now will be freely and readily available as part of the unclassified Public Records archive and suitable for an impartial assessment, then one is clearly in for some unexpected discoveries.

During the war years, any information concerning the activities of the RAF and its personnel were contained within a heavy code of secrecy. To exchange or even seek this kind of information at that time without official authority was to break the law in an offence, which could be interpreted, as treasonable. There was also a Ministry of Propaganda which was empowered to decide what information was suitable for public release in the interests of avoiding providing the enemy with useful information and of maintaining or creating a healthy degree of public morale.

Thus, in wartime Britain, one was conditioned to the reality of information being withheld, manipulated and distorted by specialists in such matters. It was an ideal situation whereby official myths could be generated and predominate. Many of the RAF's wartime activities were heavily censored by such influences. Consequently the civilian population was not aware of much that was actually going on at the time. If they were at all aware on the evidence of their own eyes, of actual developments in progress all around them, then they were wilfully prevented from knowing the framework of strategy and tactics that were involved. Where the RAF was concerned, there was tremendous activity in the massive expansion of the service, particularly while new airfields and aircraft were needed. The emergency conditions and general urgency of such matters meant that mistakes were inevitable and such a secret situation was readily exploitable by opportunists whose main interest was commercial gain. There were many get-rich-quick deals and backhanders, as Ted Stone made clear to me during the building of the airfields.

The design, layout and building of a military or civilian airfield was and still is an intricate and highly specialized construction business. As far as I know there are no text books available on it. With the number of airfields built to their design and specification, one would naturally look towards the Air Ministry records of that time. But, that is not as easy as it sounds. Many documents do not exist. One finds, some 50 years later, that there are still official means of withholding information related to that time while, at the same time, officialdom glibly talks of the 30-year rule. Yet, on consideration, this should not be really surprising. There are plenty of people still alive who witnessed such events who, if they have maintained a long and discreet silence on certain issues could, if they so chose, talk at length and in detail. And although the pointers may at first appear to be very flimsy, there are enough of them and they are of such a nature that there may well be good reason for the service authorities to go on concealing the reality of the situation even at this distance from it.

The evidence on the ground is now fast disappearing; even so, one only has to look at the evidence on a map to appreciate that so many Bomber Command airfields were badly sited, so that clear flying access was not possible as the circuits of neighbouring airfields overlapped dangerously. To remember that only a third of those airfields authorised were ever built is to begin to wonder as to just what degree of bungling inefficiency and commercial corruption were involved in those which actually were.

At the time when airfield construction in the northeast was absorbing massive supplies of priority labour and materials there were some deep and wide rumblings of scandal and fraud which even the secrecy of the time could not contain. There were one or two veiled yet persistent parliamentary questions and, these were followed by a few token court cases up and down the country for a while where directors of building and civil engineering firms were given jail sentences for defrauding the government. But, in the main, these were the small fry. They had to be. Because where airfield construction was concerned only the big boys could play. And if the government wanted its airfields building, then they had to go along with the big contractors as best they could. Not that the big firms had any need to be crudely fraudulent anyway. With the vast majority of their work on 'cost plus profits' contracts, they had a virtually open cheque for an airfield job. All they had to do was provide some convincing figures at the end of the day ... the larger the figures, the more profit they made. Apart from the peacetime RAF stations which were usually very closely supervised on quality of work, the rest were wartime only and attracted much less works supervision.

When one looks around now at the big names in building and civil engineering, so many of those with any degree of national standing in the industry can only look back to the wartime years of airfield construction as their great bonanza which made possible the industrial prowess they wield today. So while the numbers of survivors of workers actually involved at that time is now greatly diminished, they do exist in plenty. And there is no doubting that the discreet silence which is maintained by today's industrial magnates, as the heirs of the wartime airfield builders, is paralleled by an equally discreet silence, if not concealment, by today's MoD. That it should continue some 50 years after the event and the 30-year rule be revoked to support such continuing secrecy, is certainly food for thought in a country where it is customary for politicians to boast of the standards of democratic freedom which are enjoyed by one and all.

If the wartime airfield construction programme is something to be still discreetly concealed by those who govern then, more than likely, the aircraft construction programme is in close parallel. For the directors and shareholders of such firms as Short Bros, A. V. Roe, Handley Page and the like could bask smugly in public encouragement and approval for their contribution to the war effort as they enjoyed the benefits of lucrative Ministry of Supply contracts, while the statesman were applauding the successes of the *'Wings for Victory'* savings movement and periodic collection campaigns for scrap aluminium from the general public.

In thinking of the aircrews in whose memory the control tower site at Elvington is now being developed, there is a need to remember that it was against this kind of questionable and discreetly concealed commercial and financial background that the youngsters of the 1930s and 1940s found themselves subjected to the subtle social pressures of the time. So that, for anyone growing up then, or for many young adults who had known years of continual unemployment, nothing seemed more natural or attractive than to join the armed services. Among other things, it was a way of openly demonstrating one's manhood while at the same time a large official propaganda effort was going on all round them to encourage such ready recruitment. And of course, among the armed services, one of the select elite were RAF aircrew. This elitism was, as it still is today, an active part of official policy.

The prospect of flying with the RAF in any capacity at all was put forward and widely publicised as a glamorous and distinctive business. At a time when this country was under a real threat of invasion, when nightly bombing of large towns was the rule. To fly on active service with the RAF was made to appear as a ready way of doing something personally and effectively about the situation. If initially, to fly with Fighter Command was a first choice for so many; the fact remained that even with Bomber Command, one was still in a position to do something and hit back at the source of the threat, somewhere deep in enemy territory.

Young men volunteered in their thousands. Many were rejected on medical grounds or by the sifting methods of the Selection Boards and Primary Training Courses. The successful ones went forward into flying training and if each and every one had readily volunteered for such courses, then when flying training was over and operational flying was their lot, they soon learned just how glamorous the business really was and exactly what they had let themselves in for. With the action going on all around them, no-one was in a better position than they were to weigh the odds of survival from a choice of being trapped and burned alive in a crashed and blazing aircraft, being shot out of the sky by enemy fighters or anti-aircraft fire, a mid-air collision with friendly aircraft, the odds of a parachute failure on baling out or death from exposure in a wintry North Sea.

If, in their first tour of operations, they came to appreciate the odds of survival as one in three and decided to opt out of such flying activities, then they soon learned that, if they had volunteered themselves eagerly into the service, they could by no means volunteer out of it. Should they refuse to fly there was the veiled threat of a possible court martial situation or the absolute certainty of being re-graded and recorded as Lack of Moral Fibre; a social disgrace to be carried around to every Service Station and situation one was posted to. In the prevailing conditions and attitudes of the time, it was generally considered to their credit that so many accepted the risks and carried on with the job to whatever finish that fate had in store for them.

The crew of the Lancaster bomber Y -Yeoman in which Sergeant (Yorky) Millns was the rear-gunner. He is first on the left, standing, with his left hand on one of the other crew members.

From the outset the casualty figures were high. But with secrecy the watchword of all wartime activities, the reality was easily concealed by the authorities. Many of those crews who were killed over England in the earlier years were quietly interred in local churchyards. So that today one can move around so many village cemeteries in lowland Yorkshire and Lincolnshire to find those Portland headstones lined in groups in half a dozen or so among the wide variety of memorials to village folk.

It was only later, when the crash rates and casualty figures mounted so highly to become common knowledge in flying areas, regardless of official silence, and could not be effectively hidden, only then were the special interment areas set apart in the graveyards of towns and villages as war cemeteries maintainable by the Commonwealth War Graves Commission.

If official policy and publicity projected wartime aircrew members as valiant young heroes, then it is necessary to make the point that they were indeed popular among a large part of the population.

Many families had members in aircrew and, in the northern countryside; aircrew members made hosts of friends and became involved in all kinds of social activities in the villages and towns surrounding their bases. Nonetheless, there were those civilians who only saw them off duty and disapproved of their life style. So there was a measure of envy and resentment for these youngsters who had money to burn as servicemen, who spent their pay as fast as they received it, who lived only for today, for laughter and high jinks; these Brylcreem boys who had so much fuss made of them, who had the pick of the girls at dances, could go out boozing every night, could get special petrol to joy ride in cars at a time of strict rationing. There were plenty of people around in Britain at that time who had no great love for aircrew; like the farmers in Yorkshire who robbed aircrew who had crashed, some even cut off the fingers of the wounded or dead aircrew for their rings.

Royal Air Force Station,
Ludford Magna.
Market Rasen.
Lincs.

101a/509/93/P.1.   27th June.1943.

Dear Mr Millns,

I was indeed sorry to have to advise you that your Son, 1038740 Sergeant Thomas Desmond Millns, is missing from Air Operations, and it is with the sincere sympathy both of myself and entire Squadron that I write you at this time.

Your Son was the Air Gunner in an aircraft which took-off on an Operational Sortie over enemy territory, on the night of the 25/26th June. 1943, but I regret to say failed to return to base. No messages were received from the aircraft after take-off, and nothing has since been heard of it or any member of the Crew.

There is always the possibility that they may have come down by parachute or made a forced landing in enemy territory in which case news of this would take a considerable time to come through, but you will be immediately advised of any further information that is received.

Your Son will be greatly missed in the Squadron for he was not only popular, but had shown great keenness and efficiency in his work throughout the time he has been here. This was his tenth Operational Sortie over enemy territory, and his duties were always carried out with a fine courage and determination.

I feel most deeply for you at this anxious time, and we all join with you in hoping and praying that some good news will eventually come through.

Yours sincerely,

D.A. REDDICK.
Wing Commander,Commanding,
No 101 Squadron R.A.F.

Mr T. Millns.
53, Maple Drive,
Scarborough. Yorks.

The Squadron letter that was sent to the family of Sergeant Thomas Millns after Y Yeoman went missing on the night of 25-26 June 1943. The family was never told any more news.

177

So if, when their lives and possessions were being heavily threatened by enemy attack, the general civilian population made much outward show, clamour and fuss of wartime crew, although this was by no means unanimous. There were plenty who saw them only as rich pickings for easy money. Yet, if there was this measure of resentment and hostility from certain areas of the public then, if or when it was at all displayed, it was very rarely in the open. So that when Halifax Y9988 of No 1658 Heavy Conversion Unit based at Riccall in Yorkshire, crashed along the village street at Kelfield near Selby, Yorkshire on 26 February 1943 after the port-inner engine failed and, rescuers wanted to shelter the stretcher-case survivors under the only nearby roofed cover while awaiting transit to hospital, a local farmer's wife refused to have them in the house or to be involved in any way for fear of the mess. At the scene of this same crash the blackened corpse of one of the aircrew casualties was stripped of a gold wristwatch while the first rescuers on the scene were engaged elsewhere. The watch was a parental 21st birthday present of some weeks before. With York as a mecca for off duty recreation there were several cases of aircrews returning by taxi to their bases after a night out, drunk and incapable, being frisked and fleeced of all valuables, and left stranded on lonely roadsides to sober up and stagger back to base as best they could. Just as the political and service authorities lauded and feted aircrew in order to recruit and use them, so also was there a section of the public which joined in the general back slapping and approval for flying men at a time when the safety of their own skins was at risk and, as long as they could stay on hand to make some easy money from them.

As the war progressed and Bomber Command became a highly organized and effective instrument of mass destruction, there were those surviving aircrew who, if they had once had no doubts about the righteousness and value of their role, now began to doubt and question matters of policy and strategy; such issues as the whole-sale destruction of cities and the unlimited involvement of civilian populations as a result. Episodes such as the bombing of Dresden do not lie easily in the memory of those who were involved. If, over some five years, Bomber Command had demonstrably grown into a highly efficient force, mistakes of strategic planning and control abounded throughout this time.

What is so noteworthy at this distance from the events is how effectively such mistakes have been concealed by those in authority for so long. Only in comparatively recent years have the real facts of such as the Nuremberg raid been widely publicised. But, never answered. When I confronted Harris about it he said it was unimportant. When I pressed again, he said he was too old to remember. Yet, Nuremberg was Bomber Command's most disastrous raid of the war. Harris, in his book - Bomber Offensive - published just after the war, makes no mention of this most disastrous raid. Churchill in his exhaustive history of World War Two dismissed the Nuremberg raid in one short paragraph - why? The officers and politicians responsible have maintained tight lips throughout, regardless of persistent questioning; a silence which, for many of them, is now preserved so effectively by the grave.

You can read the truth about the Nuremberg raid in my book **Ghost Stations™** Germany.

There is indeed a stark contrast between the way in which so many of the young aircrew faced the prospect of death compared to the statesman and service chiefs who gave them their orders. What a spectacle so many of the latter have presented over the years as they finely steered the courses of their professional and public careers to become laden with state honours and national distinctions. How they carefully presided over the cultivation and projection of the legends of their own greatness. And how they exerted whatever covert or discreet influence they could in order to ensure that their performance and roles should be passed on to posterity with favour in the official records and histories. These eminent and honourable men, who issued the orders which sent so many to an early death, how they themselves contrived to live on and cling tenaciously to their own precious lives so that they preserved them far beyond the average span and into the realms of senility, eventually to die in the peace and quiet of their own beds.

By the time the European war had ended the civilian population was well clear of any obvious threat to their own security. In the later war years aircrew recruitment had been run down and the Empire Training Schools closed. Any volunteers in the pipeline were transferred to other services such as the army. At the same time the glamorising official publicity had ceased. On all sides there was by this time a great weariness of anything associated with war. So that, as aircrew were demobilised, they soon appreciated that they were no longer considered the wartime social attraction they once had been. Clearly the days of their elitism were over. Among civilians who did not know in any detail just what had been going on in the Armed Services, there was a widespread assumption that RAF flying personnel had had a high old time of fun and games. But with the war now over, it was now time for them to be serious and settle down to proper work like everyone else.

While grappling with some of the personal problems of initial resettlement into civilian life, ex-aircrew looked around at the strange peacetime situations in which they found themselves. They could see plenty of those who had profited from the war by staying securely at home to exploit lucrative situations like the black market in food and supplies to become financially wealthy. This was at a time when so many ex-service people were trudging wearily from one place to another seeking employment, all too aware of the great gap in their working lives, their lack of qualifications and the small number of vacancies in the high unemployment of the early post-war years. They soon learned that they were viewed as extra and unwelcome competition on the labour market.

If ex-aircrew tried to explain what they had been doing during the war years to people who clearly did not know, then so often their listeners chose to interpret such remarks as bragging. They soon displayed their distaste for such talk. Ex-service people were quickly made aware of the need to forget the war. For many of the general public it was now all over and finished with. A widespread post-war attitude soon developed that service people in general and aircrew in particular had been doing a job, a job, which they had been paid for and well paid into the bargain at that. The public did not want to know any more about it. What interested them was getting back into the swing of a life of peace and plenty.

Yet for so many, including wartime aircrew, it could not be all over. They still had private, recurring nightmares to sweat through again and again as they struggled to come to terms with the after effects of the experiences and pressures they had lived through. As they compared such experiences to the quality of their life as civilians, they soon learned that there could be no going back to what they had once known. War had drastically changed their lives. They would never be quite the same again. During those early post-war years they had plenty of opportunity to examine their lives and the validity of long-held personal attitudes, which had been readily and widely accepted during the war years.

If victory had been accepted as a common goal, somehow worth striving and risking one's life for then, for many, peace had a hollow ring about it and was something of an anti-climax, a time for re-examination and a source of self-doubt. So that if, in the later wartime years, many aircrew had had personal doubts about such activities as the mass destruction of Germany, then the post-war revelations of the Germans as people being ordinary folk rather than some distant and vague threat of evil; gave food for further consideration.

As the post-war years passed, Bomber Command's real casualty figures began to slowly emerge for the first time in public. They confirmed what aircrew themselves had known all the while from first hand, that the slaughter had been tremendous. At the time it had been accepted as part of the necessary price to pay in order to achieve the goal in view, namely, victory. Also at the time it was not possible to know the actual fate of those reported missing or failed to return. In the absence of any further details, there was always a hope of survival even if as prisoners-of-war. The end of the war was also the end of many such hopes as the facts were recorded and assembled.

Yet, with the passage of time over the years and in spite of the casualty figures, there developed a cult of armchair critics, who had never seen a shot fired in anger, who could debate and question the value of the whole Bomber Command offensive. So that, as time went by, many ex-aircrew were finding that if they themselves had personal doubts over special aspects of wartime bombing strategy in which they had been personally involved, then this was nothing compared to challenging the validity and conduct of the whole air offensive against Germany. And from such post-war influences the earlier value and meaning of their wartime efforts could only be insidiously eroded.

If one tries to examine and gauge how individual ex-aircrew attitudes were changing during those post-war years, then it is difficult to arrive at what may be typical. In examining Leonard Cheshire's periodically published and well-known views on the deterioration of personal values in the post-war situation then, with his unusually wide range of wartime experience, one could easily classify him as an extreme case; not that that necessarily invalidates or detracts from the value of what he says.

However, John Hannah, who was awarded the Victoria Cross, hit long-term ill-health and consequent unemployment problems as a civilian. This was at a time when the annual bounty for the Victoria Cross was some £10 or so. He contracted tuberculosis to die while still a young man impoverished and embittered at the post-war indifference of that same country and its people who had made so much of his wartime conduct.

How far was such a change of view typical is difficult to assess. But, for those ex-aircrew who were re-examining the value of their wartime role in the changing values of the post-war situation, a memorable development some five or six years after the ending of World War Two, was the outbreak of war in Korea.

Could they see it as any other than negation; an open demonstration of the discounting and betrayal of the value of their wartime effort by world leaders and statesman?

For those who stayed on or returned to service in the RAF to make it a career, who gained promotion and distinction in their chosen field, more than likely they can view their wartime service as part of a worthwhile experience. But for the thousands who were demobilised, who returned to their earlier jobs as accountants, shop-keepers, bank clerks, teachers, salesman and the like, to marry, have children, pursue their careers, come to terms with disability and sickness and cope with the frustrations and routine of their lot as civilians, one wonders how they really view it all now.

At the time there appeared to be no real choice. One did a job that had to be done in the light of the problems of the time. And one responded, as one was best able. But, with the cold reality of 50 years on, one wonders just how they see it today. Even so, whatever their present view, the fact remains that through the danger, threat and fear of their shared wartime experiences, so many of them came to know a rare and high degree of human awareness and friendship, something far beyond anything they had known before, the like of which many of them have never known since. So that it has become a high peak of living contained in the hectic, shared experiences of their wartime service, something they now value highly even if it can only exist today as a vivid memory.

One remembers that so many people were involved in World War Two with the aim of ensuring a better way of life and living. When one looks around with this in mind at some of the social value and issues of the present time, then clearly there is food for thought. We need only glance at the living situations in which so many of us find ourselves today with such heavy emphasis on the creation of personal comfort. First and seemingly foremost, there is our domestic accommodation and its modern conveniences such as central heating, fitted carpets and kitchens, stereo sound, colour television, the launderette, the microwave oven, the telephone, the motor car. If we then go beyond the confines of the home, there are the leisure interests of holidays in the sun or round-the-world jet travel on demand, if one can afford it. In the field of technology we have achievements such as electronics, lasers and the exploration of space. If all this is progress then what, we may well ask, are the main motives for such developments? How are they really being used other than as predominant avenues for self-indulgence, competition or aggression?

If we then turn our attention to another area of today's social issues, we have widespread drug abuse, aids, racial unrest and violence, vandalism and massive unemployment to select just a few. And if we contemplate such issues in our present day situation while remembering that, during the course of World War Two, the repeated phrase at that time was that it was for a better world and a better way of life, then we may ask ourselves whether there is anything about our present lives and ways of living today which is really worth anyone having died for 50 years ago?

We may well recall the recent fiasco in the Falklands as the latest in a long sequence of worldwide campaigns which stretch out at intervals over the whole post-war period as politicians and service chiefs, among those who order our lives, continued to play the game of brinkmanship and demonstrate that we are much closer to being involved in war than we usually care to think as with the Kuwait invasion of August 1990 which, President Bush seized as an excuse for a Gulf War.

This was nothing more than an American activated oil war. American banks had been falling faster than the Scuds. Once again it was good troops into battle. But, this was **not** our war.

On Sunday 3 February 1991, Edward Heath said: "This is the new imperialism and, I am against the new imperialism. It is not our job to go throwing our forces around the world and saying, 'This is an evil man and so on'."

I agree with Heath one hundred per cent. Before the outbreak of the Gulf War, I sent to both The Times and The European newspapers to put on record, that should there be a Gulf War, the backlash would be unthinkable, and look at what it did. Made millions homeless, set oil wells on fire and Saddam still was in power and yet many of our military now suffer due to illnesses brought on by the war in one form or another.

The Times did a Poll that showed the public in favour of the Gulf War. I did a Poll with 307 Second World War Veterans and **not** one wanted a Gulf War. It was not our war. And 85 per cent said: "What about us poor buggers from the last war trying to live on a pittance of a war pension?"

So true, look at our military lads who have been affected from the Gulf War, Bosnia, Kossovo and else where … and the thanks they get?

It all comes down to Official Mythology. Major said the Gulf War was just. Thatcher said an aggressor must not get away with it. So, what about Turkey...? Half of Cyprus is still under Turkish Military Occupation. They have been there since 1974. The reason. No oil. And there are many other countries that both you and I could mention; but no action is ever taken.

When now, considering the lasting achievements of Bomber Command and remembering some of the extreme effort, skill, courage and capacity for self-sacrifice which went into it, if one seeks to evaluate it in the light of today's events, then one is in an area of confusion, contradiction and dismay. This is all far different from the sanctimonious cant and superficial lip service, which are aired in the flowing phrases and ritualised ceremonial of remembrance and veneration just once a year for about an hour or so. In like degree the actuality of war was and still is very different from how it is now formally remembered or so often discussed or referred to.

If, at the present time, it is fashionable to question and re-question the standards of our social values, then one wonders just how many thousands of today's young people would volunteer, under any circumstances, to risk their lives in a highly dangerous situation month after month for a duration of years with little expectation of survival and with the accepted aim of preserving the life style we now have or the hope of something better. Or are today's young people too alert and astute to be persuaded or drawn into such a predicament?

Any surviving wartime aircrew member has now lived the greater span of his human life. One wonders how he now sees his wartime service in relation to the rest of his living as events have turned out. Does he now see his volunteering for service as being misguided? Does he in any way see himself as being duped, exploited and eventually discarded by those who wielded power and authority during his youth? Would he approve or encourage the young people of today to volunteer for anything as readily as he himself did years ago? Yet these are questions that one can hardly ask outright. Such issues will inevitably be painful to contemplate subjectively and a natural reaction would be to seek to avoid them. So, if one respects or admires the ideals and objectives contained in their aims and efforts as young people 50 years ago, then one can only allow them the privacy of their thoughts today.

Throughout the course of World War Two the RAF sought to project a certain image about its service and its activities, an image which would find favour and be acceptable to the general public. In the secrecy of the time there was no great problem involved. Anything which was not considered in keeping with the approved standard was simply not publicised or referred to. With all records kept by the Air Ministry it was and still is at the RAF's discretion as to who may be allowed access to them.

What now slowly emerges is that the RAF has its own ways of approving historians and scholars who wish to study the documentary records in its possession. And it would appear that it also has its own methods of vetting, if not censoring, the finished products of such research prior to publication. The basic method is so absurdly simple. If a historian refuses to respond favourable to various criticisms or observations on his work, then his future degree of access to the more sensitive and classified material will either not develop or be greatly reduced.

This of course is by no means obvious when one reads a published outline of a particular area of RAF activity. So that if one starts out in thinking that it is possible to freely examine the available evidence on an RAF subject more than 30 years after the events in order to try and arrive at a balanced and impartial assessment, one soon learns the naivety of such an approach. The RAF is not interested in balanced or impartial assessments of its activities. If it cannot now censor information as it once did during the war, then it has developed and still uses a battery of manoeuvres and techniques whereby it can still maintain tight control of what emerges. **That is the reason why no wartime airfield has been preserved and why all the aircraft were so quickly destroyed after the war. No airfield, no aircraft, no buildings. Remove the evidence, to leave only ghost airfields and ghost squadrons.**

And so one learns to appreciate, that if the official view of any aspect of RAF history is a carefully groomed or contrived one then, in the way things operate, it will, over a lengthy period of time, be the one, which apparently predominates. When that day arrives there will be no sign or mention of the number of badly sited airfields, which could never be used for aircraft, the dubious financial details of airfield construction, the serviceable aircraft that were discreetly buried as late war supplies far exceeded demand. Nor will there be any mention of closely supervised dumping of brand new and unused workshop tools and equipment in nearby rivers and others still boxed buried deep in the ground, as bases were closed.

In short a whole host of private and individual memories of questionable and unpublished official activities, anything that the authorities might find embarrassing, will have been ignored and unrecorded. The Air Historical Branch will have few problems in maintaining its present stance until such time as all the wartime survivors are gone from the scene when the depth and degree of interest in such matters will no longer be what it once was. Thankfully for those interested in objective impartiality, where RAF activities are concerned either in war or peace, there are enough autobiographical accounts from actual experience and books such as my Military Airfield books for Lincolnshire, Yorkshire and London which, are now to be brought out as the Back to Base Series.

These, and the **Ghost Station**™ Series with such stories as Z Men that is told for the first time in **Ghost Stations**™ **3** and a reply to the Z-Men by Wing Commander Ken Wallis – of 007 James Bond fame – told in **Ghost Stations**™ The Story; to challenge and question the real value of the carefully nurtured traditions of official mythology.

THE COLLEGE ROAD GHOST

"I have just finished reading your book **Ghost Stations™ III**," said Derek Smith. "I found the little bit about Hornchurch interesting as I now live very near the old Hornchurch fighter station. Also the story about Hendon for in 1957 I spent thirteen weeks at Hendon Police College which, I believe at that time used a lot of the old buildings belonging to Hendon Airfield, as a mess hall and dormitories etcetera.

"I regret to say nothing I saw in that thirteen weeks was in the least bit ghostly. However, I do have a story that happened to me when I was a child and, I thought that it was about time I told someone about it, before it gets put down to the ramblings of an old man."

Derek Smith's story is such an interesting one that I had to include it. It is not one with airfields; nevertheless, it does have some bearing, from the fact of being able to understand the reason behind the ghostly visit, in this case, the jawbone.

I would like to make clear that the house in which Derek Smith then lived, No. 19 College Road, was originally gas lit and the fittings for the electric light; were all converted gas mantles fitted to the wall. His bedroom was at the back of the house and the ceiling sloped with the roof-line. Thus, the only place for his bed was in front of the door, the window was at the foot of the bed slightly to the left.

With the scene set, let us get on with Derek's very interesting story ... Derek:

"I was born on the 11th of September 1938, in a small two-up and two-down wooden weather boarded cottage, in College Road, Epsom, Surrey. I lived in that cottage with my parents and younger sister until I was fourteen years, when we all moved to a council house on the other side of the town.

"When I was ten or eleven years old, I was helping my father to dig a plot in the garden, ready for planting, when I turned up a lower human jaw bone, complete with teeth. I cleaned it under the tap to free it of the chalky soil, which was adhering to it and, took it into the house.

"I thought no more of it, and my father said we should take it to the police the following day. I went to bed that night at my normal time and fell asleep.

"I woke up suddenly during the night, the moon was up and was shining through the small window, at the foot of my bed. In the light, standing next to my bed, which was the old fashioned kind with head and footboards and a metal frame, was the figure of a man.

"He was about five feet ten and dressed in Cavalier dress, a large hat with feather, knee breeches, a sort of short jacket or coat over his right shoulder and, a shirt with puffed sleeves. But the funny thing was that he was grey, and semi-transparent, yet he looked solid.

"I took all this in, in the few seconds that I looked at him. The only way out of my small bedroom, without touching the figure was over the headboard, which is the way I went, without taking my eyes from the figure. I hit the light switch and the figure vanished.

"I woke my parents who told me it was just the moonlight, shining through the net curtain, over my window. I did not believe them and, I do not think that they believed it either.

"The following day the jawbone was reburied deeply in the garden; and although I was frightened, I had to sleep in that bedroom for the next few years until we moved house.

"I never saw anything else in my bedroom and, although the moonlight continued to shine through my window at night, it never again took on human shape.

"I firmly believe that I saw the ghost owner of that lower jaw … and that he wanted it put back into the earth; where I presume, that the rest of his body was buried.

"My parents told nobody of my experience, so if the cottages are still there and, the area has not been redeveloped, I would think that he still lies under the ground, in the cottage garden."

AN UNCANNY OCCURRENCE

Dear Mr. Halpenny

As with your previous four books, Ghost Stations V was an interesting and thought provoking read. However, this time, one particular extract took on greater relevance as it involved my late father. What I will relate cannot be regarded as a ghost story, but it does follow the theme of unexplained occurrences.

The extract I refer to is paragraph three and four on page 94 of the article "Strange Happenings at RAF Soerabaja", beginning with "The third case concerns a transport called the Lisbon Maru."

The above is from a letter sent to me by Robert Bell from Sleaford, England. He also sent articles to support his story. Yes, as Robert Bell says, it does say on page 94 'The third case - Anthony Eden speaking in the House of Commons - concerns a transport called the Lisbon Maru which was being used to convey over 1,800 British prisoners of war from Hong Kong.'

It continues but let me return to the Robert Bell story. On Christmas Day 1941, Robert (Bertie) Bell - the father of Robert Bell who sent to me the story - was captured in Hong Kong along with other members of his regiment, the 2nd Battalion Royal Scots.

Bertie Bell signed up with the Royal Scots Unit at 18 after leaving high school in Edinburgh, and saw action on the frontiers of India long before the outbreak of the

Second World War. In 1936 he was caught in the so-called 'War of the Lemons', when the Moslems and Sikhs battled for a temple in old Lahore.

After the Japanese captured Bertie Bell in December 1941, he was held for nine months then left for Japan aboard the ill-fated Lisbon Maru. This is where we came in with Robert Bell's letter ... to continue.

Twelve hours out of Shanghai on October 1, 1942, three torpedoes struck the Lisbon Maru; and as soon as the ship was hit, the despicable Japanese battened down the hatches on the 1,740 prisoners of war aboard.

The Japs locked their prisoners in the holds and went about rescuing 2,000 of their own men who were aboard.

Fortunately the ship banked precariously on a sand bar and after 26 hours ... the only water to drink being either salt water or moisture that condensed on the bulkheads; many of the PoW's including Bertie Bell, broke out of the hold. They found the stem completely awash but a group of islands was visible about 10 miles away. Bell seized his chance and leaped into the sea and swam toward a Japanese sloop. But it picked up only Japanese and machine-gunned the allied troops. So Bertie Bell struck out for the mainland, reaching the island with about 14 other men.

For two days the natives fed them, then Jap marines rounded them up and Bertie Bell was assigned to work on the docks of Kobe and Osaka.

After the Japs surrendered, Bertie Bell was processed through Yokohama, Manila and Australia before discharge. He went to Berlin in September 1946 and ran the copy room of the press section of the British Foreign Office.

Now that you have a complete picture of both the man and his situation, let me return to the Lisbon Maru. And the time it was torpedoed in October 1942.

After escaping from the ship's hold, Bertie Bell swam for over eleven hours before reaching land ... now comes the uncanny occurrence and Bertie Bell's son, Robert Alexander, takes up the story:

"Meanwhile, thousands of miles away in Edinburgh, my grandmother awoke suddenly and turning to her husband said: ... 'our son's in danger, he's in water.'

My father explained that after the war ... his mother recounted this story to him and when they worked out the dates ... it transpired that her sudden awakening coincided with him swimming for his life."

You can read the newspaper headline about the above story on the next page. Also, I will mention this in relation to a very similar telepathy incident that happened to me.

This I explain in **Ghost Stations™** The Story

POWs Locked in as Ship Sank

JAPS locked 371 British prisoners in the hold of a torpedoed ship and in another case packed 1,300 American captives into the coal bunkers of a ferry.

The survivors of these grim experiences told their stories yesterday.

The British soldiers, captured when Hong Kong fell, were aboard the 7,000-ton Jap ship Lisbon Maru when it was torpedoed in October, 1942.

The Japs locked the soldiers in the holds and went about rescuing 2,000 of their own men who were aboard.

Not a single Jap was lost, but 870 British were drowned.

"The Japs wouldn't let us get out of the holds. We lay in them all that day after the torpedoing," survivors said in Osaka yesterday after being liberated.

"The Japs battened down the hatches and pulled a tarpaulin over us. Water started seeping in. We pumped from seven o'clock that night until nine the next morning. The only water we had to drink was moisture that condensed on the bulkheads.

"At nine on the second night there was a sudden lurch. We broke the hatches open and found that the afterpart of the ship was afloat. We jumped overboard, but were not picked up by the Japs until the next afternoon."

Salt water was all there was to drink for the 1,300 American prisoners loaded into the coal bunkers of a Jap ferry after being taken from the prison camp at Manila.

They were told they would be transferred in a few hours. Thirty-eight days later survivors, mad with thirst and near suffocation, dragged themselves up from the holds.

"It was worse than the march from Bataan," said the Americans. "Men starved to death and were beaten to death then. In the ship they suffocated and died from the heat."

A Newspaper Headline of the day.

GHOST STATIONS™ *by Bruce Barrymore Halpenny* ©

www.ghoststations.com

THE NEW GHOST STATIONS™

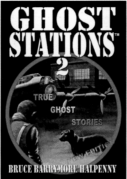

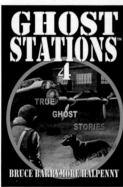

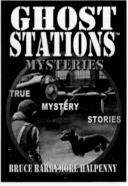

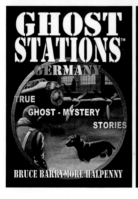

… And more to follow!!!

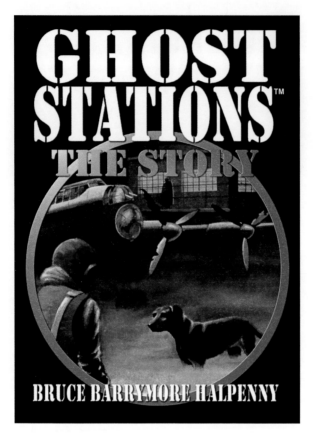

The Story about, GHOST STATIONS™, featuring special stories, photographs and a glossary of the abbreviations used in the GHOST STATIONS™ Series.
GHOST STATIONS™ The Story is a companion to the Series of GHOST STATIONS™ Books.

www.ghoststations.com